A NOT-

"A loving, nostalgic and evocative portrait of a life in a small, New England village. If you ever wished the people in Norman Rockwell's beloved paintings could speak, read this book."

MARGARET A. SALINGER,
New York Times best-selling author of Dream Catcher: A Memoir

"Every now and then a story comes along that takes us back in time. It reminds of so many wonderful details of our childhood that easily gets lost in life's shuffle. Little did we know growing up in that small town of Plainfield, New Hampshire that we were surrounded by greatness. Viola's book captures the essence of a very special small town in America that attracted world famous writers, scupltors and painters. This book will make you pause and smile as it takes you back in time in a very special place."

DEBRA DION KRISCHKE,
Co-Author of "Inspired Entrepreneurs – a Collection of Female Triumphs in Business and Life!" and "Fearless Women Fearless Wisdom"

"A Not-So-Small-Time Town brings back memories of my childhood filled with nostalgia of simpler times. Vi perfectly depicts Plainfield and the special people who made it their home. It gives all generations something on which to reflect."

RAY REED,
Upper Valley Radio Personality for Thirty Years

"Growing up in small town America during the 1950's and 1960's was a pleasant way to spend your childhood. Having lived in Plainfield, NH all of my life, it was nice to revisit that time period and view it from someone elses vantage point. On my mother's side of the family were some of the original settlers of Plainfield. This book jogged some memories of people and events from Plainfield's history"

SCOTT MACLEAY,
Owner of MacLeay Construction

A Not-So-Small-Time Town

A Not-So-Small-Time TOWN

Growing Up in Plainfield, New Hampshire

VIOLA SAWYER LUNDERVILLE

ARCHWAY PUBLISHING

Copyright © 2013 Viola Sawyer Lunderville.

All rights reserved. No part of this book may be used or reproduced by
any means, graphic, electronic, or mechanical, including photocopying,
recording, taping or by any information storage retrieval system
without the written permission of the publisher except in the case
of brief quotations embodied in critical articles and reviews.

Archway Publishing books may be ordered through booksellers or by contacting:

Archway Publishing
1663 Liberty Drive
Bloomington, IN 47403
www.archwaypublishing.com
1-(888)-242-5904

Because of the dynamic nature of the Internet, any web addresses or
links contained in this book may have changed since publication and
may no longer be valid. The views expressed in this work are solely those
of the author and do not necessarily reflect the views of the publisher,
and the publisher hereby disclaims any responsibility for them.

Any people depicted in stock imagery provided by Thinkstock are models,
and such images are being used for illustrative purposes only.

Certain stock imagery © Thinkstock.

ISBN: 978-1-4808-0057-1 (sc)
ISBN: 978-1-4808-0059-5 (hc)
ISBN: 978-1-4808-0058-8 (e)

Library of Congress Control Number: 2013905901

Printed in the United States of America

Archway Publishing rev. date: 4/8/2013

Table of Contents

In Dedication To	ix
In Thanks	xi
Introduction	xiii
A Not-So-Small-Time Town	1
Water Adventures	6
Glorious Freedoms	15
My Family	20
The Magic of Christmas	44
Spoiled Rotten	51
Many Walks of Life	54
Plainfield Families	59
Friend For Life	89
Meriden White School	103
They Are Not Just Buildings	118
The Plainfield General Store	119
The Plainfield Community Baptist Church	125
The Blow-Me-Down Grange Hall	131
The Plainfield Town Hall	134
The Mothers' and Daughters' Clubhouse	136
The Philip Read Memorial Library	138
My Furry Friends	140
My Love For Speed	143
Weekend Fun	146
A Look Ahead	158
All Goods Things Must End	160
In Special Memory	164

In Dedication To

My Loving, Children and Grandchildren

My Precious Daughter, Tracey and her devoted husband Todd

My Wonderful Son, Cory and his adoring wife Kelly

All of my Sweet and Beloved Grandchildren
Brady, Brooke, and Bryce
Brittany

Where does one as blessed as I am, begin to show the ones that I hold so dearly in my heart, how very much they are loved. I treasure everything about each of you and what you bring to my life. Thank you.

I began this story, as a way of sharing my life and the values that came from it with you. I am hoping that it gives you a good understanding of the experiences that I brought to our family, and the importance of special people in your lives, when they choose to give unselfishly of themselves.

In Thanks

My loving and patient husband, Sonny

My Parents, Ellsworth and Louise (Atwood) Sawyer, Jr.

My dearly missed sister, Carol

My Grandparents and the many generations of my ancestors and their descendants

The People of Plainfield, New Hampshire

My Friends and their families

My Teachers, Church and Civic Leaders

Peggy Salinger

My loving husband, who supports me in all of my "projects." This one entailed hours and hours, day and night. It truly became an obsession, a longing to bring all of my thoughts to life. Thank you for the beautiful family that you gave me, which led me to the desire to share my story. Our work together, has created a very special and loving family unit, with values to pass on, just like my family taught me to do.

My family, beginning with my parents, and those extending back for many generations, many of them from Plainfield, all of you have added to who I am today. We are forever powered with the love and support of family, to face all that life has to offer, good and bad. Our family really gets it.

There is no story without the people, who are Plainfield, New Hampshire. Everyone who touched my life, owns a piece of, and adds to the story, and many of you I owe a deep thank you to, for being a part of my life.

The very special people who have been so close to me, I hope that I have said it all, in what you are about to read. Thank you is not enough.

Peggy, my lifelong friend, my rock, my editor… Thank you for a lifelong friendship that has never wavered. Your support, honesty, and encouragement in this endeavor is endearing, and your expertise and skills in editing, priceless.

I love all of you, and my not-so-small-time town, Plainfield, New Hampshire.

Introduction

It is funny how we can live our lives side by side, yet each remember it a little differently, or in some cases very differently. It of course, depends on each individual's perspective, and in general their outlook on life. It is the diversity in all of us that keeps life interesting. After all, we would not all want to be "Stepford Wives," or in my story, "Stepford Children."

My writing began as a memoir to my children and grandchildren. Although over the years, my children were fortunate enough to have spent much time in Plainfield, and thankfully, shared in the closeness of our extended family, it is however, still different than growing up in the actual place. My young grandchildren love to be treated to an old-fashioned 4th of July, in my hometown, again, it's not really the same as living it. Once more, it's back to the whole idea of one's perspective.

I was filled with the desire to share with them, the small (or maybe not-so-small) town atmosphere, and the country life that I so very much enjoyed as a child. Even though, we are an extremely close family, today's way of life is very different than what I grew up with. Some of the changes have been brought on by the loss of so many loved ones from our large close-knit family, the distance between where people live which is fortunately shortened by modern day travel, and in general, a life-style which dictates a more scheduled and hectic pace of life.

As I progressed with my recalling, writing, and sharing, I realized that my story, was growing into more than my original plan. As my thoughts unfolded about past times, I was being encouraged by my dear friend, Peggy, as well as my husband, Sonny, to spread my wings a bit, and write to share my story with others who might also enjoy being nostalgic about the place, Plainfield, New Hampshire, and the times of my youth (1955-1972). Who knows, maybe others will enjoy the ride as well, especially if their life and perspective were similar to, or perhaps even very different from mine.

To make this about more than just my point of view, and to do some fact checking, I decided to visit with old friends, some visits long overdue. I am so very thankful that I had an opportunity to have a wonderful visit with Alice Jordan before she passed. I was able to thank her, share my feelings on her family's role in my life, and have a few laughs with her. My husband and I, had a lovely evening in the home of Scott MacLeay, where he and I, and his dad, Don, recalled the grand days on the hill and beyond. Jean LaPan Temple, welcomed me into her beautiful new home, where we shared lunch, and the memories of the good old days. Many of which I have shared, a few we will keep to ourselves.

I spoke with Peter Berry, and his sister, Debbie Berry Maville, who I had not seen in many years. We relived some fond and sad moments. It was also nice to reconnect with Joyce McNamara Judy. Mary-Jo Barto Straus, now lives in Florida, so we burned up the lines between there and New Hampshire. While wintering in Florida, I called back north, to speak and revisit old times with Lee Raymond Carey. Maybe, I did those two things backwards. Debra Dion Krischke and Sherry Martin Mascovitz, also shared lively memories with me via the land line. My ongoing relationship with the Chellis family provides a continuous connection to some very special people. Ray Reed, thanks for the information and excitement over my endeavor. Steve and Donna Beaupré offered historical timelines, and shared a couple of chuckles with me. My family, whose brains I picked, on an ongoing basis, helped me to keep the family and town history straight. My mom, Louise Atwood Sawyer, my great-aunts, Kate Read Wilder Gauthier, who is sadly no longer with us, Jean Read Hebert, Emma Towne Mosher, my great-uncle Albert "Abe" Read III, who is also missed, and my aunt (really my dad's cousin, but so special to me that I call her aunt), Carolyn Daley Ziemba, all have provided me with a wealth of memories and knowledge in this endeavor. My cousins, Bev Wilder Widger, Mike Sutherland, Joyce Read, Mabel Rogers Prescott, and Linda Shepard Stone, have been patient and loving, while I challenged their recall. The ongoing and renewed relationships that I have experienced during this process, has been the biggest reward for me. I hope you enjoy reading about this journey back in time, as much as, I have enjoyed writing it.

A Not-So-Small-Time Town
Growing Up in Plainfield, New Hampshire

On a beautiful spring morning in 1955, my life began and so did the onset of my growing-up years in Plainfield, New Hampshire, a not-so-small-time town. To some, Plainfield, a small town whose residents live a rural country lifestyle, may seem like a setting with little to offer. However, to me, the town offered countless experiences that created the basis of who I would become, and these experiences have served me well throughout my life.

For years, I have jotted down notes about this charming town and that formative period of time in my life. I soon began to realize, as I progressed with the writing process--using the old-fashioned method of putting pencil to paper--just how many thoughts and memories occupied my mind.

Plainfield, New Hampshire, has been a very special place since the time that it began. It is a beautiful town, occupying nearly fifty-three square miles of land and water. Its western edge lies along the banks of the Connecticut River. There are fertile fields lying among the rolling hills and the stately mountains, which all add their picturesque qualities to the scene.

Mount Ascutney rises majestically from the land in the neighboring state of Vermont and watches dutifully over the river valley. This mountain, called a monadnock, reaches over three thousand feet, featuring forms created during the last glacial period. Huge sections of its mighty granite outcrops can be seen, especially near the top. Many photographers and artists have captured the mountain's beauty in their works, including Plainfield artist Maxfield Parrish. The deep and rich blue-green colors painting its slopes change with the variations of light that shine down on it, while the clouds that hover above offer their shadows to the peaks and valleys, adding to the picture before you.

In autumn, Mt. Ascutney's sides light up like a fire with glorious shades of red, orange, and yellow. The exploding colors create an alluring New England sight that brings many from afar to see. The winter snow will soon begin to cover the peaks and signal the approach of the next season. Each direction traveled gives the viewer a different perspective of the mountain's elusive apex. On approach from roads in both New Hampshire and its neighbor, Vermont, one's eyes see what appears to be the tallest peak only to soon discover another reaching higher and claiming its place as the summit. I still search eagerly for which peak of this grand landmark is the highest, even though I already know the answer.

The charm of this serene river valley life offers nature's very best and has beckoned many dating back to the time of King George. In 1761, King George issued a land grant to settlers living in the town of Plainfield, Connecticut, to begin a new life on the untouched, fertile grounds of this region, where the Connecticut River flows through the valley. The Connecticut is the longest river in New England. It runs four hundred and seven miles from its origin in the Connecticut Lakes in northern New Hampshire, where it borders Canada and eventually sheds its clean waters into the Atlantic Ocean at Long Island Sound in the state of Connecticut.

The Connecticut River, as well as the brooks and streams feeding it created a generous water supply for the settlers and their animals. They had found a perfect place to settle next to a vital waterway, which was bordered by land containing rich soils needed for farming and raising sheep. This land also provided a bountiful supply of exceptionally fine white pines that could be used to build ship masts for the king's English fleets.

Where did all of this natural beauty and rich, fertile land come from? It is best described as a geological paradise created when the last glacial period occurred during the Lake Wisconsin Glaciation dating back nearly twenty thousand years. After reaching its final extent, the Laurentide Ice Sheet started to recede northward, and the Great Lake Hitchcock began forming near Middletown, Connecticut. This was due to the damming up of the abutting ice margin near Rocky Hill, Connecticut.

The glacial lake grew as the ice slowly melted and retreated up the Connecticut River Valley, carving the land and leaving in its path a magnificent landscape. As the water leveled, it deposited its fine silt and wondrous clay along the way. These valuable deposits continue to provide richness to the valley today. All of this splendid geological history created unique and prosperous lands for its future inhabitants and the setting for my story.

During the late 1800's, Plainfield and the neighboring town of Cornish became the summer home--and in some cases, the residence--for many famous artists, architects, writers, lawyers, and politicians. This would come to be known as the Cornish Colony. Drawn by the natural beauty, these artists and intellectuals sought solace from the bustle of city life. Among those who came was the sculptor, Augustus Saint-Gaudens, whose home and studios are now a National Historic Site and Park. This property was first owned by a lawyer, Charles Beaman, Jr., who also established the nearby Blow-Me-Down Farm. He was seen as being responsible for the beginning of the Cornish Colony, as he had introduced Saint-Gaudens to the area.

Others soon began to follow to be near the famous sculptor, and they too, were amazed at and inspired by the beauty of the river valley. The names of those seeking the qualities of the land

and proximity to Saint-Gaudens include world-famous sculptor Hebert Adams, playwright Louis E. Shipman, and Charles Platt, a painter and architect. Stephen Parrish, an etcher, and his famous son, Maxfield Parrish, illustrator and painter, also made Plainfield their home. President Woodrow Wilson established his summer White House at the Harlakenden House on the Plainfield-Cornish town line from 1913-1915.

Also bringing their talents to the area while enjoying the beauty of the land were Winston Churchill (the writer, not the politician); Philip Littell, a writer; Percy MacKaye, who was a poet and dramatist; George Rublee, a lawyer and a diplomat; and actress Ethel Barrymore. In the early 1950's, author J.D. Salinger found his seclusion in the woods of this special place. His discovery of this beautiful river valley turned out to be a wonderful addition to my life, as his daughter, Peggy (Margaret) and I became lifelong friends.

I know this sounds like a Who's Who bragging list, but it is far from a complete roll of names. There were many others who sought out the splendor of this area. My hope is that the reader will come to see the richness of what Plainfield, and the surrounding area brought to the lives of these important people in the same manner that it brought prosperity to the townspeople. Also important to the story, is that those who came from the city were instrumental in helping to form the cultural history of this area, which in turn influenced future generations, including mine.

The members of the Cornish Colony not only offered cultural growth to those living in the Connecticut River Valley, but they also provided a needed boost to the economy. Some of the city people (so called by the locals) traveling to the area boarded in the homes of the townspeople during their stay. Additionally, they purchased local products and hired numerous people from the area for a variety of jobs to help them maintain their large homes and properties.

Generations ago, my family was also attracted to this beautiful countryside. I wish that I could hear the accounts of their first impressions when they arrived. Fortunately for me, the generations continued to make Plainfield, their home, and it eventually became mine. More than a hundred years after my first ancestors settled here, I, too, was able to revel in the bounty of the natural resources of this rich river valley in an era that allowed me to just be a kid.

I spent my youth exploring, learning, and growing up while enjoying a simple lifestyle full of freedom, memorable places, and special times. I was loved and nurtured by a large family; however, there were many others who touched my life and are also a vital part of my story about our unique small town of Plainfield. To me, this wonderful place was not so small-time, but extremely big and rich in all that it had to offer me.

Water Adventures

Like the settlers of Plainfield discovered, the natural water sources have continued to be an important aspect of Plainfield's history throughout time. Winding through this beautiful countryside are various brooks and streams. Spring-fed ponds are also found laying among the tall white pines. I'm sure that children from each generation dating back to the early years have enjoyed swimming in these waters, and the kids sharing the days of my childhood were no different.

Every spring, as soon as Mother Nature cooperated, we headed for a swimming hole. There was no lack of great swimming holes, each unique in its own way, from the depth of the hole to the seclusion of its location, and of course by who hung out there. With the exception of a few homes, there were no swimming pools to frolic in and certainly no community pool. We had to use what nature provided for us--cold, clear brooks and streams that widen and deepen just enough in certain areas, especially at a twisting bend in the stream. Sometimes we would swim in ponds of varying sizes and depths. These waters were also home to frogs, fish, and often snapping turtles, as well as pondweed, lilies, and cat-tails which lined the ponds' bottoms and banks.

Just as I had my favorite holes, I know that other kids in town also had their choice spots to swim. There were many places to chose from. Each one had a little village aspect to it, which was based on the proximity of the hole to the homes where the kids and their gang of friends lived. When visiting friends, each of which, have a place in my story, I was fortunate to be able to share in their special swimming hole. While in the Village of Meriden, visiting with the Gibson's, I swam with them and other Meriden kids in the Blood's Brook, by the covered Mill Bridge. Our next door neighbors, the Eaton's, had a man-made pond where I and other kids swam, when their grandchildren were visiting. The Jordan family on top of Westgate Road owned a pond where my family spent a lot of time swimming and picnicking with their family in this private spot.

My family enjoyed many outings to Mascoma Lake, aside the Shaker Bridge in Enfield, New Hampshire, as well as at my great-uncle Norman's camp on the same lake. We delighted in our trips to the Townsend Dam in Vermont, especially one very memorable outing that you will hear more about later. Kennedy Pond in Windsor, Vermont, was another favorite of mine. When I took swimming lessons there, I felt like I was in the big leagues, with the lengthy docks built over the water and certified lifeguards on duty. Trips to Plummer's camp on Crystal Lake, also in Enfield, gave me a chance to hang out with the older kids and were a special treat. My family's rare, but glorious treks to Hampton Beach on the Atlantic shore, were of course, the very best.

The closest thing that we had to a community swimming area was MacLeay's pond. Don and Vera MacLeay, long-time residents of Plainfield, always had the community's interests at heart. Therefore, they opened their man-made pond to the local kids. Don owned a construction business and built a large spring-fed pond down back of their home. The pond, being approximately three-quarters of an acre in size, was huge compared to the other swimming holes available to us. I haven't visited it since I was a teenager; I wonder if its size would live up to my memories. The pond was cold, deep and murky due to the natural clay bottom, created by the geological past. On approach, you could see the different colors of the clay bottom that were reflected to the top of the water, there was a brilliant turquoise hue in spots and a bluish-gray look to others. Other ponds with muddy, dirt bottoms, lacking these beautiful clays, do not have the same look.

There were many lazy, yet playful, hot summer afternoons spent with my friends, Scott and Danny MacLeay, Mary-Jo Barto, Lee Raymond, Shirley Stone, and scores of others who frequented this welcome spot. One of our favorite things to do, was to jump off the anchored raft in the middle of the pond and see if we could touch the bottom with our feet, fifteen feet below the water's surface. Reaching the cold, mucky clay was both exhilarating and a little scary. We also loved to swing off of the rope hanging from the large construction boom on the north side of the pond. The boom was so high up, that we had to use a ladder to climb up and grab the rope.

Swimming classes were held at this pond, where I and others gave town-sponsored lessons to the younger children who were eager to become swimmers. I was fortunate to have earned my Senior Lifesaving Certificate during my summer stays at the 4-H camp in Bear Brook State Park in Suncook, New Hampshire. I hope other past campers can remember our wonderful water instructor, Ms. Livingston "Livy"? You better have had your swimmer's ID tag on the correct side of that board which indicated if you were in or out of the water, or you were in big trouble! How about a Polar Bear swim? Anyone want to visit Vesper Rock with me?

The Blow-Me-Down Brook, which bordered my parent's property, was a great source for perfect swimming holes. Some of these holes were easily accessible through fields, others were more deeply hidden in the woods. The Blow-Me-Down begins as a watershed from Croydon Mountain and forms in a dammed area in the neighboring location of Cornish Flat, in the eastern part of Cornish. The brook continues its nearly thirteen mile long winding path through the town of Plainfield, then back into Cornish on its western edge, where it serves as a tributary to the Connecticut River. The swimming hole nearest to me, and the one that I used most frequently, was located in the field right below my home. This field was owned by John Meyette, another vital member of our community. John's field was also the site for fun-filled field day events sponsored by the all-volunteer fire department, where the young could enjoy games and events such as: three-legged races, sack races, two-person wheelbarrow races, bobbing for apples and pie eating contests--my specialty.

This frequently used swimming hole was located a few hundred yards in from Westgate Road, and it was a choice spot for us kids to meet at and cool off in. Back in the day, the hole was deep enough to dive into from a large, weatherworn tree limb that had fallen and lay hung out over the water. I can still see, in my mind's eye, this limb right down to the protruding, forked branch stub, which extended from the end of it. To get to this swimming hole in the brook, you had to descend down a pretty steep bank that had well trodden paths down to the water's edge. We also used the bank to sit on while we pulled off the numerous bloodsuckers from our body parts, that those nasty creatures had stuck to during our time in the water. Sometimes, we would venture downstream to explore the many treasures created by nature that the brook and woods would have to offer us in our travels. I especially remember the way the tree branches hung low over some sections, making it feel secretive and tropical, like traveling in a far away jungle that I had read and dreamed about. There were beautiful yellow pebbles that lay along the brook's bed which added to the clarity of the water, where you could easily view the life of the minnows, trout, and plants thriving below.

On the opposite side of Westgate Road, just below our home, there were more fields, where great wild raspberry bushes grew. These fields lay between our road and the twin bridges on Daniels Road, and led me to another exciting spot that my friends and I used to cool off in from the warm summer sun. Hidden from the adult world and found only by traveling rock-lined paths winding through the woods, this spot had a wonderful veil of secrecy around it. A group of us met and swam there on a regular basis. You announced your presence both on approach and as a response from the hole with a shrill sound, something between a whistle and a vocal sound that had no meaning to anyone but us. Shirley Stone had a great sound, we always knew exactly who was there when she let go. At this spot, we dove off from a white birch tree branch that hung above the water into the somewhat shallow brook below. Remembering now that I am an adult with children and grandchildren, the thought of this amazes me and scares me silly. I can't imagine that it was ever deep enough for this risky practice, "by the Grace of God, no broken necks."

On occasion I swam in a small hole about one-half of a mile downstream from the John Meyette hole, that lay under the Hayward Road bridge. It was a small hole that was used by the Clayton Morse family who lived across from this spot. In later years, this home was lived in by more friends, the Dow family. I would also join Richard Dow, his cousin Bill Kelly, and other kids from this area who hung out there for an afternoon of swimming fun.

Traveling a mile or so further south down the Blow-Me-Down, there was yet, another small hole hidden behind a tall, thick, layer of bushes. It was a short walk off from Thrasher Road through a field laying on the left, just before the Bishop home. The brook ran very lazily along this stretch, twisting around slow bends in its bank. Unlike the other holes, this was not a popular spot where my daily swimming buddies went. This was a special place where I swam many times with the Fitts Family. Dear, Mrs. Evelyn Fitts, loved to gather us girls up--her daughters, Gail and Mary, and myself, and off we'd go to swim. This group of teen friends was a little older than my normal hang-out group. I was around eight years old at this time. My cousin, Bev Wilder, who by the way had a great in-ground pool at her home, the Cassidy girls, the West girls, Kathy Martin, Coleen Wilder, and others would join us from time to time.

Just a short distance down the Blow-Me-Down from the Fitt's swimming hole, on the right side of the road by a small bridge, was a popular swimming hole, that I often yearned to go to, known as Thrasher's. It's deepness and thrilling tire swing attracted kids from all around, not to mention the older boys who hung out there, among them, the Riley brothers and Lee Baker. The feeling of swinging wildly out over the water in an old, over-sized tire was exciting, yet nerve wracking. I always had a pit in my stomach just before letting go of the swing and jumping into the water below. I was not allowed to go to this hole as liberally as I was the others. Was it the tire swing or the older boys?

Other brooks in the area also offered great places to swim. The Ledges were legendary. Located just over the Lebanon town line, on the Trues Brook Road heading towards Meriden, were The Ledges. Amongst the steep, rock-cliff banks were large boulders. They had wide, flat shelf-like surfaces jutting out where you could dive off from or jump from into the swirling pools of water below. Their powers drew teens from all over the area, Plainfield, Meriden, Lebanon, and beyond. They held for me the stiff warning from my parents, that they were OFF LIMITS, NO EXCEPTIONS! I can truly say that I obeyed this rule with only one exception, when I was in high school, and "everyone" was going there after school. I followed the crowd. I guess, I just couldn't be left out this one time.

Perhaps time has erased my failings, or I really followed the spirit of the rule on this one visit. Because even though, I recall walking on the forbidden grounds, somehow I don't remember ever stepping a foot into the water. However, vivid in my mind are the many times that my friends headed to The Ledges without me.

The Blow-Me-Down Brook also held other adventures for us kids to take part in. Each spring, we anxiously awaited for the delivery of new trout stocked by the Fish and Game truck, they often delivered the fish to the brook, near the bridge just below our house, so I had a bird's eye view. The telephone party line would begin to hum with the news of the deposit, and out would come the fishing poles, bobs, nets, and of course the worms, especially the almighty night crawlers.

I had a little side business of selling fishing worms, so I became quite the "expert" at digging earthworms and hunting for night crawlers. This technique required the following: cans filled with dirt, a flashlight, a quick hand, and lots of patience. I patrolled the lawn at night with my flashlight and when a crawler slithered out of the soil, I would quickly grab it, then pull gently so as to not break the worm in half, and at last the prize was mine. The best time to go hunting for night crawlers was after it had rained. I also earned some spending money by catching minnows in a trap, that once they swam into it, there was no escape. I had the trap tied to a tree where I would then lower it into the brook and check it daily for my catch. I hauled the minnows by the pail-full, up the path on the steep bank, that led to my house, where I stored them in a washtub until I sold them.

I can't say that my abilities were as adept at the fishing hole, because I spent a lot of time untangling my hook, line, and sinker from just about everything around me such as, the brush lining the brook, and even the overhead trees. Trips into the cold water during early spring to untangle your line from the rocks is not much fun either. However, fishing was still a good time. Besides trout, the brook was also home to hornpout, which were a little tricky to deal with. They are a member of the catfish family and their large mouths are surrounded by whiskery-looking barbels. I may still have a few holes in my hands where the hornpout angrily pricked me while I was trying to take them off the hook.

The local ponds also offered good fishing. Next door to my house, Mr. Eaton had his pond stocked from time to time, and he welcomed the neighborhood kids to come and fish in it. If we got bored of fishing; there was always skipping stones and seeing whose stone would skip the most times and go the furthest. If you were lucky and you found the very best flat, slim, smooth stone, it would skip all the way across the water to the other side. We might have done a little skinny-dipping in the pond, too. That was always a cure for boredom.

Another source of excitement, was tubing down the brook on old inner tubes that were used in tires and usually had been patched in several places. We would start at one of the swimming holes and follow the flow of the water as far as we could or dared to go. Sometimes, we discovered ourselves a couple of miles downstream. We would have to get off of the tubes in areas where the water was too shallow to carry us and wade forward to deeper water, especially if we were riding on bigger tubes. The tubes came in various sizes, depending on the type of tire they had come from. The huge tubes from tractors and construction machines were great in the ponds for just floating around. They could hold several of us at once. We would rock them back and forth trying to knock each off and then get back on by swimming underwater and up through the center.

In the winter, the Blow-Me-Down offered an exciting, yet challenging place to ice skate. Like on tubes, we would also try to get as far as we could downstream on the long stretches of frozen water wearing our ice skates. We would have to work our way around the areas that could not be skated over due to open waters or thin ice. So, we would walk the bank until it was safe and then skate our way forward. We had to carry our boots with us, as sometimes, it would be quite a distance between open waters and the next stretch of solid ice. Occasionally, we needed our boots to get back to our starting point, unless we decided to skate our way back upstream.

The ponds made great skating rinks, except that they had to be shoveled off. Everyone would grab a snow shovel and clear the ice while skating. We had night skating parties; gliding and slicing across the ice on a cold, clear, starry night was quite magical. The older teenage boys would build a bonfire in the snow, where we could warm our hands and toes. I burnt a lot of socks and mittens over the years. I think I seared a boot or two, as well. There is nothing like roasted hot dogs on sticks, toasted marshmallows, and smores cooked over an open fire. Once in awhile, I would enjoy going to skate on the lighted, man-made, outdoor rinks in Windsor or Lebanon, but there is no comparison to those special times with my friends under the stars, on what Mother Nature had already provided for us.

Glorious Freedoms

Like the hours that I spent at the swimming holes, most of my days were filled with periods of freedom that carried over into other pastimes as well. My version of freedom, and also for many of my friends from this era, meant that I had large amounts of unsupervised time. There were very few restrictions on the distances that I could travel to while enjoying the latitudes afforded by this special time in my life. We lived in pretty simple times, at least through a child's eyes. Whether we were headed off to the swimming hole or a day of exploration, our instructions were pretty basic--finish your chores, don't swim alone, and be back by supper time. I'm sure that our parents were concerned about our safety, but they somehow also had the ability to let us have a great deal of independence in our daily lives.

I spent hours roaming and exploring the vast woodlands, sometimes by myself, and sometimes these explorations were shared with friends. I knew like the back of my hand; the woods, the streams, old abandoned roads and paths, stone walls, abandoned wells, distinctive stands of trees, and the lone wooden giants standing watch over the woods and fields. One of my favorite spots to explore, was the ruins from a fire at an old estate hidden deep in the woods across from the Hodgeman home. The long, abandoned drive ran along the edge of a pasture near my grandparent's former farm, where they were living at the time of the fire, in the mid 1950's. The only signs left of the tragedy were the cellar hole and a large fireplace standing on one end of this once grand home. I traveled over these areas in all seasons, even the deep snow was mastered using snowshoes built by my grandfather Sawyer. My only fear, was the dreaded, occasional snake that slithered its way onto my path, or perhaps I onto its path. No fear of meeting strangers, no fear of getting lost.

Not every experience was completely carefree however. My friend, Jean LaPan and I, may have had a little close call one day. We were walking to her house on a cold, fall afternoon when a man went by in a large, dark colored car, with out-of-state plates. He was singing "Beautiful Dreamer" at the top of his lungs, so loudly we heard him on his approach. We thought it would be funny to mock him, so we did. He drove by us very slowly and stared us down. We were so afraid that he would return and of what he might do to us, that we jumped over a bank and hid under leaves. He did make a couple of trips back and forth, then drove off laughing. We hid there for a long time. I had on a new pair of mittens, that I left behind in the leaves. "Where are those new mittens that I just bought you?" I was forever losing my mittens. Jean and I found them in the spring, not looking quite so new.

I rode on horseback as often as possible, traveling the back dirt roads of Plainfield and Cornish, sometimes with friends, many times solo. The back roads offered long stretches of desolate miles, with homes few and far between. It was such a feeling of tranquility to be so free. As a teenager, I rode these same back roads in my boyfriend, Geoffrey's, open jeep sharing with him the same sense of carefree excitement. My parents must have worried about me being on my own so much and wandering in extremely remote areas. I can't imagine that in today's world, that I would be allowed such freedom.

The long afternoons after school also held periods of time filled with the light-heartedness of youth. Whether my friends and I were walking home, or already deeply involved in whatever adventure we had planned, it was time that was ours. Of course, we all had our homework to complete and the standard household chores to do, but we worked together and quickly our tasks were behind us. When I mention standard chores, I mean like feeding the family pets, clearing the table and washing the dishes, which were small daily tasks that most kids had. There were also big chores that had to be completed on a regular basis by some of my friends. These were not once in a while tasks, but daily hard labor chores that were required in order to maintain a farm, or some other family business. Many of my friends fed and cleaned up after animals both before, and after school. The older kids might even have had milking chores to do. If they lived on a big farm they didn't often get to go to other kid's houses to play, if their friends wanted to play with them, they went to the farm and helped them out.

One of my weekly chores was ironing the huge basket of clothes, everything in those days needed ironing; sheets, table clothes, handkerchiefs, and list went on and on. However, before they could be ironed they had to be washed. I also often helped my mother with the wash, not by using a washer with all of today's modern conveniences. We had an old wringer washer that fortunately had an electric motor, which ran the agitator, pump, and ringer. It took the following steps to perform the task at hand; pulling the washed clothes from the open wash tub, which had been filled with a hose, and feed them one piece of clothing at a time through the wringer mechanism attached to the tub. Thanks to modern day electronics, we did not have to crank the wringer, but it was still a tough task to pull those heavy wet clothes out of the hot water and lift them up into the wringer, all the while, trying very hard not to get a finger or two involved also. Of course, the whole process had to be repeated with the rinse; pump out the dirty wash water, fill the tub with clean rinse water, agitate, and then begin the rigorous wringing process again. In winter, this task was done at the kitchen sink, the summers afforded us the chance to be outdoors on the porch. Much nicer! Then, the clothes were hung out on the line to dry. Wintertime, not so nice! Your fingers really can freeze to the clothesline. Additionally, the clothes did not dry, they froze solid, so we brought the stiff articles of clothing in and hung them over anything you could find to dry them on. By the way, have you ever ironed clothes not dried in a dryer? Just dampen them with water, shaken from an old soda bottle that was stopped up with a metal sprinkler head on a cork base. Also, the towels were not so fluffy soft, when they came off the clothesline. The first modern washer and dryer to enter our home in the late 1960's, was a cause for celebration. Do you remember the bonus towels and glasses that came in the large boxes of some laundry detergents?

Another modern invention that we got in later years, was the portable dishwasher. I couldn't wait to use it, no more having to wash and dry the dishes by hand. Yippy! Then came the instructions for using it: open up the top, take out the top rack, fill the bottom rack with the dirty dishes, put the top rack back in and fill it, hook up the hose to the faucet, hang the pump hose securely over the side of sink, and be sure to be around during the pumping out cycle, because if you forgot the securely part, "Holy Moly!" Finally plug it in and let her rip. I don't remember the dishwasher having a drying cycle either. Did it really make things easier?

I wonder about the youth of today, especially during the elementary years, who have no time to just be a child, explore, and imagine. Every moment of every day, is packed with a schedule of events meant to occupy their time and fulfill their every need. Children now also have every electronic device known to man, to fill in any extra moments that they might have free. I had a transistor radio, a small red Regency TR-1 with a leather case. It really only came in clearly at night, when I would fall asleep with it under my pillow listening to WPTR 1540 out of Albany, New York. I still have it, I just might try and see if WPTR is still broadcasting tonight as I fall asleep. My old radio might be a cure for menopausal insomnia. My family also had <u>one</u> TV, which when the weather was good, aired three stations. Our first color RCA TV came into the house in the mid 1960's. Wow! Now we could watch, in color, some of our favorites, like <u>Bonanza</u>, or <u>The Ed Sullivan Show</u> with the cute little mouse, Topo Gigio. Ed Sullivan also brought us the debut of the "<u>The Beatles' British</u> Invasion," singing those great hits like, "She Loves You." I really wanted to hold Ringo's hand, after all, he was a drummer like me. OH YES, <u>The Wonderful World of Walt Disney</u>, was also now in color, just how wonderful is that. <u>Dark Shadows</u>, my afternoon soap opera, was thankfully still in black and white.

Even darkness did not curtail our freedoms. We walked back and forth, between each other's homes on those dark country roads, lit only by the stars and the moon. The night sounds of the high-pitched peepers singing in unison from the frog pond just down the road, the hoot of the owls as they pierced the darkness with their bright shiny eyes searching for prey, the gentle breeze rustling the leaves on the tree branches, and even the call of a wild animal were the normal and welcome signs of the life surrounding us. I only feared what might be lurking in a nearby, abandoned old barn. I also dreaded that the scary, imagined barn scene would show up in my dreams once again, and disturb my sleep. I now worry that the youth of today may have much bigger concerns disturbing their sleep. I think about today's life with deep trepidation. Are those times of glorious freedoms gone forever?

My Family

Although the times, that I spent with my friends or in solitary pursuit of my freedoms amongst our beautiful landscape were very important to me, my extensive family was also a source of much richness in those days. Time spent with family, was a major part of life during these years. My immediate family consisted of my father, Ellsworth Sawyer, Jr., nicknamed "Sonny" or "Tiny" as some called him, my mother Louise (Atwood) Sawyer, and my baby sister, Carol Frances, who was nearly ten years my junior and my only sibling. In 1954, my mother's parents gave about an acre of land to my parents as a wedding gift. This land lay alongside Westgate Road and was bordered by the Blow-Me-Down Brook, with the remaining edges being surrounded by the farmland owned by my grandparents in Plainfield. The property was located on a hill making it a part of the glacial terrain, that was geographically difficult to build on; but it had a spring-fed well, that delivered cold, fresh water in bountiful amounts by using nature's gravity. In the late 1950's, my parents bought a small pink and white trailer which was situated on the upper portion of the lot. We lived in this tiny home until the mid 1960's. My parent's then had a small, modest home built on the lower section of the property, near the bank that led sharply down to the Blow-Me-Down Brook. The bank was lined with tall, beautiful white pines.

While I'm sharing this part of my early life in the small trailer, it reminds me of the charming Edwin M. Knowles children's china tea set that originally belonged to my mother as a young girl. I played often with that delicate, precious set, which I still have today, and is still fortunately in fine shape. Like many young girls in that stage of life, I held tea parties for my friends, that is the imaginary ones. Except, on this one particular morning, when I decided to surprise my sleeping mother with a real cup of tea, and proceeded to spill the boiling water all over the top of my thighs. My burns required a visit to the emergency room and leaves me with small reminders of the event, even these many years later.

This was an era that offered time to spend with relatives, not just on special occasions, but on a regular basis. It was just part of the normal routine. My youth was blessed by so many special loved ones. The full strength of my relationships with my extended family provided me with a great deal of love and support. The intrinsic values that they shared, helped to develop and nurture not only mine, but all of the generations. Even though my father's family mostly lived outside of Plainfield, they still were essential in our lives and we spent many hours in their homes and they in ours. My father grew up in Bridgewater, Vermont. His paternal grandparents, Fayette and Eva (Peck) Sawyer, owned The Sunnyside Tourist Home where they entertained guests from throughout the United States, as well as Canada and Mexico. My father was born in this home, where his parents first lived with my great-grandparents. My great-grandfather died before I was born. My great-grandmother traveled a lot when I was young, before she settled in Lebanon, New Hampshire, therefore I referred to her as my "Nana Faraway." Over the years she had several little Pomeranian dogs and she called each one, Chi Chi. Her trailer was filled with interesting knick knacks that she had collected over the years, most memorable to me a crescent moon, which unfortunately burned in a fire at her home in the 1960's. Although there was a lot of damage from the fire, luckily the family photos and memorabilia were saved, and I still cherish them today. "Nana Faraway" was famous for her wig, which she always managed to wear backwards at all big events, such as graduations and weddings. It certainly was a fashion statement.

My father's maternal grandparents, Charles and Mary (Morrison) Mosher, originated in Canada, where my father's mother (Verna) was also born, one of seven children. My great-grandparents separated in 1922, and my great-grandfather continued to live in Canada and went on to have another twelve children with his next wife. You did notice, that I said that they were separated, not divorced. I could write another chapter on his bigamy, but perhaps I'll skip that. My great-grandmother Mosher (called Nana Mosher) migrated to the United States and brought my grandmother with her. They went to live on a farm in Hartford, Vermont, co-owned by Everett Hutchins, who I and others called , "Grandpa Mick" (so-called as Nana Mosher used to live on his farm). This farm was previously owned by the Daley family and Timothy A. Daley, was the other co-owner of the farm with "Grandpa Mick." Tim was the husband of Goldie, who was one of Nana Mosher's daughters. My great-nana Mosher died before I was born, but my family still took trips to this farm which sat high on a hilltop and was difficult to access. There were two ways into the farm, one road led to "Grandpa Mick's" farm by entering through another person's farm, which was located on the River Road, in the bordering town of White River Junction, Vermont. This road leading to his farm started in their barnyard, and went up over a steep hillside left by the glacial period. However, my family usually traveled to his farm by taking a small dirt road off of Route 5 in Hartford. This dirt road also served as the driveway to the radio station WVTR (later known as WNHV), where we would stop at, on our way through to the farm. We stopped to visit with our friend and former neighbor, Ray Reed, who was busy working as an announcer at the radio station. Ray's voice would become an icon for

Upper Valley radio, he was widely listened to for many years. We then continued on our way to visit "Grandpa Mick" by winding our way through the fields and woods along this dirt road. The road was "subject to bars and gates," which meant that you had to open the bar gates to pass through various sections of the road, and then stop and close them after you had passed through. This practice was used to prevent any livestock pasturing in the fields from getting loose. I found this all very fascinating. Occasionally, we used another such road by Lionel Tracy's farm in Cornish. This road "subject to bars and gates" connected Slade Hill Road and Dingleton Hill. It wasn't an open road that was used for traveling any longer, but I would often beg my father to please take this road home while returning from Windsor, Vermont. "Please, ask Mr. Tracy if we can pass through." As you can see, the little things in life pleased me.

When "Grandpa Mick's" large farmhouse burned down in the early 1930's, he took up residence in a small section of the barn and he became the sole owner and occupant of the farm. His very simple room was warmed by a wood stove, also used to cook his meals. I can still see and smell his old blue metal coffee pot brewing on the stove. All of the aromas mixed together in that small space had a unique scent, smoky and teaming with farm life. Not distasteful, just memorable. His bed was covered with old wool blankets, probably woven at the Bridgewater Woolen Mill. Seating was at a premium, there were two wooden chairs at a small table and then wherever else you could find a spot-- on the bed, on an old wooden box, or perhaps atop a pile of grain bags. Orderliness and cleanliness were not the order of the day, he had cigar boxes piled high everywhere, which housed his treasures and his money. My special treasure was a simple wooden doll bed, made by his hands, it was covered by a thin mattress and quilt made by Great-Nana Mosher. This quilt is not as bright and colorful as you might imagine, but very simply made from scraps of plain cloth. My dolly went with me on each and every trip so that she could sleep in that special bed. In later years, he gave me these precious items to take home with me. I still have these very special gifts. The quilt now covers my treasured toy cradle kept for my daughter, and now granddaughter to enjoy. The bed frame is too old and brittle to play with. When visiting the farm, my cousin Linda and I would play dolls on a blanket spread out by the ornate stone porch steps of the burned down farmhouse. These steps were the only remaining sign of its once grand presence. In this same spot, our family also shared a picnic lunch on each trip to the farm. Nana Sawyer (my father's mother), knew how to pack a picnic basket full of delicious treats. Winter trips were out of the question due to difficult passage ways into the farm.

You can no longer access this property by the former radio station, although parts of the road remained until a recent recreational center was built there. Interstate 91 now runs through the previous green pastures that held the "old bars and gates." Also, until the recent construction, you could still see the radio tower sitting just behind the interstate's southbound rest stop in Hartford. A short while ago, I visited the matriarch of the farm on the River Road, where you could access the other road leading to his farm. She remembered "Grandpa Mick" and sadly reported to me that the old barn had also succumbed to fire and that the stone steps had been broken up and plowed under. She said that the property, as it once looked, is now indistinguishable. Only rows of field corn now occupy this very lovely spot. I would love just one more picnic there, with its beautiful view of the Connecticut River Valley.

My father's parents, Ellsworth Sawyer, Sr., "Jack" and Verna Jean (Mosher) Sawyer, first lived in Bridgewater, Vermont, and worked at the Bridgewater Woolen Mill. Like Nana Sawyer, my middle name is also Jean. My father was their only child. My grandfather was also an only child, so he really understood me as an only child for the nearly ten years before my sister was born. I was thrilled to be in his company. He loved to take me places and show me things of interest to him. On occasion, he took me to the woolen mill to visit some of his friends and to show me what he used to do for work. My ears can still hear the loud clanging of the carding machines and the running water from the Ottauquechee River used to clean the wool. This process emitted a distinctive smell that one doesn't soon forget. The smell was something like that of a room full of dirty, wet dogs--only stronger. The dye room was filled with sights of the many dark colors used to dye the wool.

In 1959, my grandparents, packed up everything, including their faithful dog Sport, that loved me unconditionally, and they moved to Woodstock, Vermont, into their newly purchased New Moon trailer. Their trailer sat on a small lot on Pleasant Street next to the Suburban Propane store. My grandfather was now managing and delivering propane from this store with Mrs. Doubleday, who ably oversaw the office operations. Talk about distinctive smells, that odor from the propane gas still fills my nostrils. I did love to ride on Grandpa's truck while he made his deliveries to the various homes located in the towns and on the long dirt roads in the hills of Vermont. On one of these trips, I decided to drive the truck which was parked at the top of a very long, steep driveway. Have I mentioned that my grandfather was quite athletic?

In the winter, Grandpa would treat me to sips of sap from maple trees. The sap was being collected in metal buckets that were hanging from the trees, that lined his delivery routes. The fresh sap was an icy cold drink that was clear and refreshing. It would soon be collected from the buckets and be made into delicious maple syrup. I also couldn't wait to stop at the old, original Woodstock Inn, where I could visit the donkeys housed in the livery stables located at the rear of the Inn. As one does occasionally, I began to question myself about this experience. Why would donkeys be kept at the Woodstock Inn? I was fortunate to have been put in touch with Dale Johnson. As a teenager, Dale worked at the Inn in the stables for the Ferguson's, who were the stable's managers during that time period. Yes indeed, there were about twenty donkeys housed in the stables in the late 1950's to the early 1960's.

My grandparent's New Moon trailer was small, but homey. Have you ever seen the 1953 movie "The Long, Long Trailer" starring Lucille Ball and Desi Arnaz? The movie is a comedy, based on their honeymoon travels with their New Moon trailer. Just as Lucy loved her cute home, my mind fondly travels back to my days of playing in my grandparent's cozy home. Nana had a bag full of colored clothespins that would occupy many of my hours with imaginative play. My imagination also gave me a special "friend" Charlie to play with. My make-believe friend, was named Charlie, after Nana and Grandpa's talking parakeet. Charlie's vocabulary was quite prolific. It was told, that once, when their minister called upon Nana, that he abruptly left when Charlie repeated a few sayings that were a little too "colorful" for the minister's likings.

My nana loved to shop! Going shopping in those times did not mean let's go to the mall, not even a small strip mall. Where the West Lebanon malls sit today in the river valley, there were once fields running open and wide. Back then, we shopped in small specialty shops located on the main streets or around town commons. We also frequented the variety chain stores like Woolworth's and J.J. Newberry's, which offered a wider selection of the more common items. Nana's favorite stores were in Claremont, New Hampshire. Friday night shopping on Pleasant Street was the place to be. The street was lined with specialty shops and the Queen Shop was at the top of my nana's list. My number one choice was the Toy Castle, also in Claremont.

Located in Lebanon, the town just north of Plainfield, was the super department store of this era. It sat at the bottom of a very large, downhill, dirt parking lot, with its name, ROCKDALE, largely displayed in red letters lining the roof line. The entire store was several football fields in length consisting of several connected buildings. You entered the first wooden building through an entrance on one end and then began the search for your wanted items passing building by building, with each doorway between them opening up to a new department. Some of the buildings were lined with shelves that would reach ceiling high and that were stocked full of every kind of imaginable merchandise. Other rooms held countless bins that were chock full of gadgets to rummage through. Whatever your need was, Rockdale had it. My favorite, of course, was the building where all the coveted toys were displayed, opening wide the eyes of all, young and old, as you walked through the door to that wonderland of play things. I can still feel my anxiousness as a young child. It seemed like it would take hours, to walk from building to building along the long wavy, wooden floor boards, that would eventually lead us to the entrance of that magical room.

Christmas time at Rockdale was a very delightful experience. They began displaying their Christmas merchandise much closer to the holiday than in today's market. When does the season begin now, right after Labor Day? The start of this merry holiday was a highly anticipated time for people from the nearby towns along the New Hampshire and Vermont border. Upon entering Rockdale, the beautiful and colorful stringed lights danced brightly before my eyes, and my ears would welcome the Christmas Carols playing joyfully over the crackly PA system. The angel hair and silver tinsel glistened on the trees set up for display. My spirits were high as

Santa welcomed me and the other children onto his lap so that we could eagerly tell him how good we had been, and to share our wish list with him. A list that was quite modest in comparison to today's lists.

There was a new doll coming to town and Little Miss Viola wanted it. The first Barbie doll was released in 1959, with the signature black and white striped bathing suit. Nana and Grandpa Sawyer took me to Rockdale to buy this doll for my fourth birthday. When they were first sold, the purchase price was around three dollars. Barbie came with a brunette or blonde pony tail, which at some point in time I decided to cut off, to give her a new look--by the way she was bald under that ponytail.

I could write an entire book on the wonderful times that I spent with my grandparents. I'll share a few more of those special memories, that may differ from other's childhood experiences. Bill Green's Rare Bird and Animal Farm located in Fairlee, Vermont, offered a close-up look at many exotic animals that one might not picture as being often seen in rural New England. My grandparents knew just how special this place was. The animals, some of which performed acts, a look inside the large Indian teepee and a walk through the crooked little house were all attractions not to be missed during a visit to this very unique farm.

Nana and I liked to take walks together. In Woodstock, a regular spot was down a little dirt road near their trailer. There was an old bed spring on the side of the road, where we would stop and throw stones through the spring's wired pattern, perhaps this was our version of an arcade or a carnival game. Later years in Queeche, another road found us at a watering trough, where the fresh water ran steadily down the mountainside, unless there had been a long drought. The fresh spring water was captured in a metal pipe that filled the usually overflowing cement basin used to hold the water.

We would stop at the trough to refresh ourselves and Buddy, their new dog. Buddy was a very large, boxer-like beast, that definitely was walking us and not the other way around. When Buddy sat in my grandfather's lap, you couldn't even see my grandpa because he was completely covered by his big pal, Buddy. There were other such "watering holes" (not pubs) in our area that my family used to collect our drinking water from. One trough was located on Route 12-A, just over the Lebanon town line, and another was in Plainfield on the Stage Road, between the Hendrick and Ward homes. Families like mine, used these springs to draw fresh water from, especially during dry times, as these springs rarely ran dry. When our well was low, we drew water from the Blow-Me-Down brook and stored it in milk cans for our daily household use. However, we got our drinking water at these mountain troughs. This cool, clear water source was very refreshing. I don't think that the springs were ever inspected and we didn't treat the water for any organisms, but we all survived.

The Mosher-Sawyer family burial plots, are located in The Mountain View Cemetery, in Bridgewater, Vermont. The plots are situated on a hillside that was terraced by my grandfather. They overlook the scenic Vermont hills displaying their glorious seasonal changes. My grandparents took great pride in caring for this sacred place. Nana, with her very green thumb built a beautiful flower garden and my grandfather meticulously cared for the grounds, including the neighboring plots, if they needed care. This was a routine, but never mundane task and was always accompanied by a bountiful picnic lunch. Our lunch was usually topped off on the way home with a visit to the White Cottage Snack Bar in Woodstock, for ice cream. I couldn't wait until that glistening white, crushed rock parking lot came into view. "We're here!" Today, when I visit the gravesites there are signs that deer and wild turkeys regularly visit this place of tranquility, which shamefully is only tended to a couple of times a year now. Sorry Grandpa and Nana, I'll try to do better.

Another spot, that my nana and grandpa liked to go to on a Sunday, was the Wilder Dam, near Hanover, New Hampshire. It was fun to walk the bridge over the dam and look down at the rushing water when the dam was open. There was a wooded picnic area on a steep bank, across the road from the dam. Like on most of our adventures, a picnic basket, well-stocked with preparations made with love, by Nana, was placed in the trunk of their car to be enjoyed on our jaunts. So, after we had seen enough of the dam, over we would go to a picnic table to eat. On one such trip, my father, who liked to wear light tan khaki pants on our Sunday outings, decided to sit on the cool ground with his food. Unfortunately for him, and us, someone else had previously walked their dog in the very same spot. We went home shortly thereafter.

In my teen years, my grandparents moved to Quechee, Vermont. Like at their previous home, I enjoyed my visits with them. I found many friends in this new neighborhood, young and old, including a special young man, Larry. My grandparents always took great pride in their home and yard. Nana built huge flower beds that colored their yard from spring to fall. She watered them from a well that my grandfather had dug, after finding the perfect spot using a dowsing stick. My grandpa happily tinkered in his workshop building unique and useful things, including my prized wizard bike. I'll take you for a ride on it later. I wish that my son-in-law, Todd, could have had the chance to know him. Like Grandpa, Todd can fix, build, or concoct anything. They would have had a lot of fun tinkering on things together.

Nana had seven siblings, three of which I never met. Those that I did not have a chance to meet were her brothers, Cecil and Stanley Mosher, and her sister Alma (Mosher) Moulton. My great-aunt Jessie (Mosher) Stevens and I, rarely saw each other, but we communicated by mail. My great-aunt Goldie, who was very special to me, was married to Tim Daley, co-owner of "Grandpa Mick's" farm, where Tim and Goldie lived when they were first married. They later moved to Springfield, Massachusetts, where Tim started a masonry construction business with their sons. They had five children: Alan, Paul, Dean, Carolyn, and Joyce. My family visited Aunt Goldie and her children's families as often as possible. It was a long trip from Plainfield to Springfield on old Route 5, before there was interstate travel in our area. I eagerly awaited a chance to play with my cousins. Their families also traveled north to visit with us. Once in awhile, when traveling to Springfield, my parent's would plan side trips to fun places like: Mountain Park in Holyoke, Forest Park in Springfield, or the thrilling and legendary amusement park of the area, Agawam's Riverside Park. On my fifteenth birthday, they surprised me with a visit to Riverside Park to see "Little Joe Cartwright," Michael Landon, from the TV show, <u>Bonanza</u>. Yes indeed, he was very cute in person, too.

 I was very close to Nana's youngest sibling, my great-uncle Carroll, and his wife, Emma (Towne)(Shepard). They also made their home in my beloved Plainfield, with their children Arthur, Gladys, Charlotte, Fredus, Joan and Linda. I spent many hours in their home, especially with Linda who babysat for me. She wasn't just my babysitter or cousin, she was my playmate and friend. Although she was a few years older than me, just as we did at "Grandpa Mick's," we played dolls by the hour in a cozy little alcove next to her bedroom. She read <u>Eloise</u> over and over again to me, and played her accordion upon my request. Outdoors, we made pretend homes from pine needles in the woods on top of the bank that rose sharply behind their house. This was also the site where the local Girl Scouts practiced their survival skills. We swam together in the waters of the Blow-Me-Down Brook, that also ran shallowly past their home. We often swam with other kids from the areas of Hell Hollow and Kenyon Hill, including the Woodley, Meyette, Decoteau, and White children. During the winter, we built snow forts on the front lawn amongst the Christmas decorations. Our family closeness has continued through the years, including trips with my husband and our children, to my great-uncle and aunt's winter residence in Florida, on Anna Marie Island.

Compared to my father's family, my mother's is very large, with several generations of relatives that were born in and made their homes in the Connecticut Valley, on both sides of the river, in New Hampshire and Vermont. Many members of my mother's side of the family also made Plainfield their home. I am fortunate to have known, and have fond memories of my family dating back to my great-great-grandmother, as I was a fifth generation baby. Therefore, I have a lot to share, about all of the generations that have touched my life. My mother's maternal great-grandparents, Fred and Addie (Round) Rogers, lived in Meriden, a village of Plainfield. He died before I was born. My memories of my great-great-grandmother revolve around family reunions and sadly her death. In that time, bodies were laid to rest in the home's parlor for viewing. So, at age six, I had now witnessed my second body laid to rest in the parlor of her last home, that sat diagonally across the road from the Meriden Grange Hall. My great-grandfather was my first viewing of a dead person. Although I suffered no long term effects from these experiences, it has certainly been a lifelong memory.

This is a good place to talk about family reunions. Today, when you speak of family reunions, most think of social gatherings, where their family gets together to see relatives that they haven't seen for awhile. Our Rogers family reunions had a somewhat different atmosphere. We too, saw some relatives not seen in while, but many of them lived fairly local, and saw each other frequently. Many of these reunions were held at the Meriden Grange Hall. This large two and half story framed hall was built in 1910, by the Meriden Grange No.151, with donated lumber from a building on the Cloverland Farm, then owned by my great-great-grandparents, Fred and Addie Rogers. The Rogers family reunions involved large meals prepared by the women and were laid out like a king's feast. These meals were followed by an important business meeting where official minutes were recorded. The family reunion business meetings were held on the second floor, where attached to the rear wall, was a metal tube fire escape. Before the meeting was opened in due form, the children were excused to go play. The metal tube made a great place to play in, however the noise generated by our many pairs of feet and generous laughter, disturbed the elders conducting their business. I remember "quietly" climbing up the fire tube in stocking feet after we had been counseled on the importance of the business at hand. Really? What kind of business could they possibly be conducting? This reunion went by the wayside sometime in the 1970's. I guess there was no more "big business" to conduct.

When I was growing up, my great-grandparents, on my mother's maternal side, Palmer C. Sr. and Lena (Rogers) Read, lived on the Read Family farm in Plainfield. This farmhouse was built by my great-great-great-grandfather Albert K. Read I. When Albert I married his wife Sophrona (sometimes also called Sophronia or Sophie) Palmer in 1843, they went to live on this farmland, which was then owned by her family. In the mid 1880's, the original farmhouse burned, and Albert I built the farmhouse that still exists today. It sits on the hillside as you are leaving Plainfield, traveling north. A picture perfect view of Mt. Ascutney can be seen from this homestead. Their son, Albert Read II and his wife, my namesake, Elizabeth

Viola (Clark) Read, were the next generation to make their home on this farm.

Following next, were my great-grandparents (Palmer C., Sr. and Lena Read), who raised their seven children in this home. Generations of grandchildren have found love on this farm, including mine. I watched (Great) Grammy Read working in her kitchen over her big stove, while I sat at the large wooden table that held in its center an old, large Lazy Susan. It was filled full of condiments and tableware ready for the next meal and all those who would gather around it. She also worked at her spinning wheel; the whirl of the wheel and the motion of her hands is ever present to me. This is not a vision that my children or grandchildren will likely ever see. Even though they were no longer in use, thanks to my great-grandparent's modern thinking and running water, the trips outback to see the "two holer" (the toilet of the time), were not something that I enjoyed. I guess the elders thought it was a hoot to remind us youngsters of the "good ole days", when they were young. My grandmother Atwood (my mother's mother), also used to break out the chamber pots during visits to her home, to enlighten us grandchildren about what is was like when she was a young girl. Is that thing really under my bed?

My great-grandfather Read, was a tall, ruggedly built man with a wide lap to sit on. I wonder how many times I pondered that large mole on the side of his face. His death in 1960, was my first visit, at the age of five, to the front parlor of their farmhouse for the viewing of a lost loved one. His life ended from a heart attack that he suffered while doing what he loved to do, hunting with his boys.

Their eldest child, my great-aunt Ada and her husband Jim Smith, lived out west with their children, Sheila and Anita, so contact with them was limited. However, my grandmother's other siblings were all a significant part of my childhood. Like with my father's family, I am pleased to be able to title them all great, because they truly were. I was always anxious to visit their homes and play with my cousins, who were in fact, my mother's cousins. I was the oldest great-grandchild out of an eventual forty-six, and my mother was the oldest member of her generation. Therefore, I was closer to her generation of cousins in age, so they were just called my cousins. We did not assign titles of generation to each other, such as once-removed and so forth.

The youngest of my grandmother's siblings, my great-aunt Jean and her husband, Bob Hebert, made their home in Keene, New Hampshire, with their two sons, Donald and Philip. I always looked forward to our family visits to their home. During our son Cory's youth, he also enjoyed staying at their home while attending a basketball camp that was directed by my cousin, Philip, who taught school and coached sports. In later years, when Cory was the Sergeant of the Guard at the Tomb of the Unknown Soldier, in Arlington National Cemetery, he treated Philip and his students who were on a class trip, to a VIP tour of the site. The family circle continues.

My great-aunt, Phyllis, and her husband, Claude S. Sutherland, lived in the Virginia suburbs of Washington, DC, with their only child, Mike(Claude R). Mike later married Mary-Lou (McIntosh), and they were blessed with three daughters. Even though there was some physical distance between our families, it never separated us. The road was well traveled both ways. They helped Cory and our new daughter-in-law Kelly, get settled and connected in the Washington area, when he was stationed there. Where would we be without family?

My great-uncle, Albert III (Abe) Read, and his wife Kitty (Kathleen Philbrick), once a model for Maxfield Parrish, lived with their five children, Cindy, Joyce, Linda, Faith, and Albert IV, on farms in the area. They first lived on Black Hill in West Lebanon and then later in Claremont, New Hampshire. Many Read family reunions were held at their homes over the years and continue today, at the beautifully situated home that they built during their retirement years, in the northern pasture of the Read homestead. Mike and Mary-Lou are now nestled comfortably in this home. Their view of Mt. Ascutney is outrageously breath-taking.

My great-uncle, Palmer C. (June) Read, Jr. and his wife Lucille (Plamondon), and their two children, Richard (Dick) and Janet, also made their home on the family farm. They originally shared the house with my great-grandparents (P. C., Sr. and Lena) until their deaths. Then later, June and Lucille once again shared the house with their son Dick and his wife, also named Janet (Dawson). Dick and Janet's daughter, Terri and her family, as well, built their home on this property. The Read farm has seen six generations of Reads, who have made their home on this land, extending over a period of about one hundred and seventy years.

My great-aunt, Kate, was the matriarch of our family for many years. She and her first husband, Norman Wilder originally lived with their two daughters, Nancy and Beverly across from the Plainfield Cemetery. In 1960, they purchased the Burrows home, overlooking the corner of Route 12-A and Thrasher Road. Uncle Norman had a wooden pallet business which was located in an old barn, that sat on a lot just a short distance south of their home. This barn was a part of the property, that was earlier known, as the Churchill Inn. My cousin, Beverly and I, played dolls, especially Barbies in her new, pretty bedroom. What a Barbie collection she had! Their in-ground pool entertained us on hot summer days and nights. After we swam, we snacked in their large, screened gazebo that protected us from the mosquitoes that were wishing to snack on us. My great-aunt and uncle threw some lively parties in their finished basement.

This well-equipped room would give any party hall a run for its money. I indeed, do have pictures of my grandmother Atwood and my great-aunt Kate dancing on the countertops-- sporting lingerie, which is fortunately in their hands, and not on. "The family who plays together, stays together." After her husband Norman passed, my great-aunt was later remarried to Raymond Gauthier. He shared her zest for life, so the party continued on. Good Times! Family Fun! Much Love! The very best support system, ever!

My mother's parents, May Viola (Read) and Francis Atwood, eloped and kept their marriage secret for a period time. During this short time of their hidden marriage, my grandmother still lived with her parents on the Read farm. There were two children born from their marriage, my mother, Louise, and her brother, Caleb Francis Atwood.

When their marriage was no longer a secret, my grandparents, first lived in Woodstock, Vermont, where his family was located. A quick note here about my maternal grandfather's family. His parents, Edwin and Mabel (Boynton) Atwood, were both deceased before I was born. Sadly, I did not have much contact with his siblings. I rarely saw my grandfather's brother, Harold (Doc) and his wife, Ruth (Brewer) Atwood. His sister, also named, Ruth (Atwood) was married to Herman Rogers (brother to my great-grandmother Lena Rogers Read, on my mother's maternal side of the family). They lived in Meriden and attended family functions and reunions, so we had more contact. There was another sister, Elna (Atwood) Drury, who later remarried and carried the last name, Putnam. I really never knew her. In addition to the Rogers reunions, where "big business" was conducted, and the Read family reunions, my parents and I, also attended the Atwood Family reunions, where I had a chance to play with those cousins.

On May 18, 1937, my grandparents, bought a farm sitting on two hundred and twenty-three acres in the not-so-small-time town, Plainfield, from Grace (Mrs. Wesley) Jordan. They lived and farmed on this property until 1959, when they purchased a farm in Westminster, Vermont, with my mother's brother, Caleb and his wife, Becky (Griggs). They bought the Westminster property in preparation for my grandparent's retirement and my uncle's eventual take over of the farm operation. During my very young years, the time that I spent on the Plainfield farm, not far from my home, was very dear to me. Even though, I was very young, my memory is sharp about my early years. There were plenty of areas on the farm to enjoy while visiting with my grandparents. While I was playing outside, I could go to the barn and see the animals or wade in the pond that my grandfather had built. Inside, my grandmother's kitchen was always filled with wonderful smells, such as bacon frying and fresh bread baking. I occupied myself by the hour in the neat little cupboard passage-way that ran from the dining room to the front hall. It is where my toys were stored and it was just big enough to play in, for a tot of my size. In my grandparents' bedroom sat an ornate floor length mirror on a marble stand, where I would sit and ponder my beauty or so I hoped. "Mirror, Mirror on the wall. Who's the fairest of them all?" This mirror now stands in my front hall for my granddaughter Brooke, to dream into.

Life on a farm offers many avenues of fun for the innovative at heart, most of them dangerous. Playing amongst livestock, farm machinery, storage areas for the various crops, and even performing standard chores, all came with warnings of potential consequences if you did not follow the rules: stay off of the machinery, keep out of the hay barn and silo, and don't play around the livestock's feet.

I felt at home in the barn during chores and milking time, which took hours, twice daily. My grandparent's milked, the old-fashioned way, milking their cows by hand while sitting on a low, small milking stool. The milk was squeezed from the cow's teats into large, metal milking pails, which when full, were emptied into milk cans. The ten gallon milk cans were the ones most commonly used by farmers. These very heavy metal cans, with metal handles on each side near the top, were covered by a heavy, metal plug top that fit down into the narrow neck of the can. The cans then had to be carried (sometimes pulled on an old wooden flatbed cart), now full of milk, to the milk room and then hefted up and placed down into a water bath, where the warm milk could be cooled down and kept cool. The milk was stored this way until the arrival of the milk truck that would collect the milk from the farms. The farmers had their names embossed onto the metal cans to be sure that the cans they owned were returned to them when the milk truck returned. My mother tells me that before the milk truck came to the farm, my grandfather had to deliver the full cans to another farm owned by Ralph Jordan, in the village.

In later years, the milk collection process was modernized by using a milking vacuum station, instead of by hand into a pail. The vacuum station sucked the milk from the cows into an attached container that was vacuum sealed. When the milking was completed, it had to be emptied and reattached to the next cow. The collected milk was again lugged to the milk room and now poured into a bulk milk cooler. Here, the milk was stirred with an agitator, the milk's heat was removed through an evaporating system, and kept cool for storage until the arrival of the milk truck. I remember my grandfather cleaning the vacuum stations and the cooler, but I can't remember exactly how it was done or how often that it was required. There was a lot of very hot water involved. This process was easier, but still a lot of work. Then more technology came. A pumping system was invented that was attached to the cows udder and then the system would suction the milk from the cows and send it by pipeline, directly to the milk room's bulk cooler to be properly stored. Milking time was certainly shorter.

My favorite chores revolved around caring for the calves. There was a powdered milk substitute which was mixed with warm water and fed to the calves in buckets with a built-in nipple. The calves would latch onto those pails so hard, that it was hard to pull their mouths off, even when the pails were empty. It's no wonder. The mixture smelled so good, they must have wanted more. I loved the smell of this concoction so much, that I was tempted to try it myself. Even through my very young eyes, I can still see them hard at work on their farm, assisted by Walt Leech, their farmhand, who roomed above their kitchen and greeted me with a big "Hello there, Trooper," when he entered Gram's kitchen from his back staircase.

I, like most children, let my curiosity get the better of me one day in the yard. I decided to pick some flowers from Gram's hydrangea bushes, which unfortunately for me, turned out to be home to a nest full of hornets. You have never seen so many stings or tears. Thankfully, I wasn't allergic.

I was fortunate to be able to continue to play on this farm for many years to come. The Farnsworth family, Henry and Dora, and their children bought the farm from my grandparents. Their eldest child, Henry was my age and we were classmates. Recently, Peggy reminded me that Henry and I, had kind of a love/hate relationship going on. He also had a cute cousin, Freddie, who came to visit from time to time. Henry, Sr., was a commercial fisherman and spent much of his time off of the farm. Dora ran the operation with the help of all of her children, both in the home and on the farm. In January of 1962, the old farmhouse burnt to the ground and they moved into the small cottage situated on the property. This cottage, had been the home to Wendell and Dot Reed, and their four children. The Reed family had lived in this home for years, dating back to the time that my grandparents owned the farm. I also spent many hours of playtime with their family, both while they lived on the farm, and in their future homes. My mind reaches back to the Wayne Newton Christmas Special, running on the TV in their living room of that farm cottage. All of us kids were huddled together watching the show with the wonders of the season flashing on the screen before us.

The Farnsworths eventually built by hand, a sturdy log cabin home to live in. They were a great team, and I was lucky to have shared time with their hard-working family.

My uncle Caleb and his wife, Becky, had four children: Kelly, Bryan, Sherry, and Joey (Caleb Joseph). As my cousins, and I grew older, we became more adventurous and fearless and the new farm in Westminster, Vermont, offered many new and exciting areas to explore. Like the other warnings that I had received, this farm had many: stay away from the railroad tracks--a track ran through the middle of the farm, don't play in the hay barn, stay away from the bulls, keep out of the sawdust bin, never, ever go into the silo, and don't ride the manure gutter cleaners-- which was an all time favorite. Who cared about a little cow poop on your sneakers when you could ride that baby the whole length of the barn until you were caught. The bulls had nose rings which were so irresistible. We'd see if we could touch the ring and then get away without upsetting the bull. Didn't our young minds realize that the adults used those rings to create pain, in order to control the bulls. It was done by putting pressure on the nose of the bull with a twist of the ring. Yikes! The hay barn, sawdust bins, and silo were all places that kids could get buried under the tons of weight from the unstable piles of products stored in each of them. However, the hay barn was so much fun to hide in, even with the constant itching caused by the hay chaff, we still couldn't resist it. The sawdust bin was a super place to slide in; the cool, damp sawdust would fill your clothes so full, that they had to be taken off and shaken out while trying to get the irritating pieces of sawdust out of all your crevices. Have you ever smelled silage? If so, then you understand why a trip to the silo was irresistible. Sometimes, I wished that I was bovine, so that I could have nibbled on those corn morsels myself. I wonder how my grandfather got any work done, he was so busy saying, "Go on with you now, you little rascals, get out of here." Did you know that registered cows have names? They are all given names. Smiley was my cow, or so I thought. This handsome, mostly white in color, gentle giant, let me ride her like a horse. Yee Haw!

My cousins and I, did have one serious accident in the barn. The cow barn was large and had a spacious manger area where a sizeable grain wagon was kept. This very large, heavy metal wagon sat on wheels located under the center part of it. The wagon could be tipped to each side to make it easier to feed the grain into the cow's troughs laying before their stanchions. Like we had done so many, many times before, all of us kids, tried to pile into the tipsy wagon amongst the grain that was left over from the last feeding. Only this time, the wagon tipped over onto my cousin Bryan's, small foot. The weight of that heavy metal wagon combined with the grain, and all of us in it, slammed down onto his foot and trapped it between the sharp edge of the wagon and the cement floor. The amount of blood that came out of his shoe was terrifying. My uncle and dad, made a lightning fast trip with poor little Bryan, to the hospital's emergency room in nearby Bellows Falls, Vermont. Thankfully, there was no permanent damage. The grain wagon was never played in again.

Like my other grandparents, Grandpa and Grammy Atwood, also liked to go on picnics. Wait until you hear this hoot. After Interstate 91 opened, there was a rest area near exit 5, on the southbound side. We would pack up the picnic basket, and all of us, usually including my uncle's family, would head to the rest stop's wooded picnic area to enjoy our wonderful meal. We all thought that this was the greatest thing. A rest stop on the interstate? I wonder if anyone, not traveling somewhere, does this today? There are probably better spots to choose for a family picnic.

As at my other grandparents' home, I was fortunate to make new friends and meet cute boys living next door, in this case, his name was Johnny. I also was able to experience the world beyond Plainfield. As always, at the end of the visit, I eagerly returned to my not-so-small-time town.

The Magic of Christmas

Christmas has always been a very important time in my life. My family celebrated this and every holiday in a splendid way. Splendid for us, did not mean fancy or outlandish, as my family did not have the extra money to spend. However, we were very rich in family and tradition.

The Christmas season didn't begin months early, like it does now. It officially started after Thanksgiving, a holiday that was also celebrated with a large family gathering. The Thanksgiving meal, filled with dishes prepared from old family recipes, was usually held at Grandpa and Grammy Atwood's home and was shared by all members from both sides of the family.

When the Christmas season was upon us, the stores would be brightly decorated, Christmas music playing joyfully over the loudspeaker, and the excitement would build. "Be good! Santa is watching for good boys and girls." One sign of Christmas, was the star that lit up the hillside in Cornish, just as you approached the Cornish-Windsor Covered Bridge. How I hoped that we would be taking a night trip to Windsor soon, so that I could look up the power line and search for that beautiful shining star. You would often catch glimpses of it as you started down the long stretch of Route 12-A, running parallel to the Connecticut River. I was also eager, each Easter to see the magnificent cross displayed at the same sight. Some twenty years later, my children also began searching in excitement and anticipation for those twinkling lights during those holiday seasons. It was all so magical. How did they light up? I recently discovered that they were placed there by Armand Vezina, a local man from Windsor, in the early 1950's. His son, Ronald, recalled to me that his father built, by hand, these symbols. His father worked for the local power company and was given permission by the company to install them. He placed the symbols on the top pole of the power line that ran up the steep hillside in Cornish, overlooking the Town of Windsor. The lights ran on a timer during the appropriate holidays. Eventually, Mr. Vezina was unable to sustain the upkeep of this project. Sadly, those beautiful lights no longer glow for the eager eyes of the young and the old.

In the early years, our Christmas tree was carefully selected in the woods on my grandparents' farm. With the cold winter air making our cheeks and noses red, we would traipse through the deep snow with the sun bouncing off its icy surface, to search for the perfect tree sitting amongst the hundreds to pick from. The chosen one, was just waiting for little Viola to claim it, bring it home and decorate it. My father would skillfully chop the tree down. Then, he would drag it back through the snowy terrain and out to the road to be tied to the roof of the car, where it lay safely secured for its trip home, to take its place of honor in our living room. Why do they always look so perfect in the woods and not quite so perfect in the tree stand? After my grandparents sold their farm, we had to pick our tree out from a local vendor, which was somehow never as exciting. Upon our arrival home, the tree would be set up in an old three-legged cast iron tree stand with the short screws that never held the tree up straight. Invariably, we would have to run a string from the top of the tree and secure it to a curtain rod or whatever else would keep it right side up. How many times did we get the tree all trimmed, only to have it lean heavily to one side?

Decorating the tree was always a magical time, with Christmas Carols playing on the Hi-Fi stereo. "I'm Dreaming of a White

Christmas…" The decorations were old familiar ones used year after year; the metal bells, the delicate, hand-painted glass ornaments, my plastic parakeet in honor of Nana's bird, Charlie, and in later years those precious ones that my sister Carol and I, had lovingly made over time. The stringed lights were the old small, ribbed, colored bulbs with pointed tips. They burned so hot that great care had to taken when placing them on the tree. My favorite lights were the bubblers with the fat, colorful base and the colored water that would bubble up the long slender candle. The lights were made even prettier with the addition of the oh so treacherous angel hair, made of spun glass, that we mounded onto the tree. I'm still itching from those days. Topping of the trimmings, were the silver strands of glittering tinsel, that we meticulously placed on the tree, strand by strand, until we tired of the mundane job and just threw the remaining pieces on in clumps. Last, but not least, we topped off the tree with a beautiful shining star. The end result, was nothing less than a splendidly decked tree gloriously twinkling away, waiting for gifts to be placed below its laden branches and some special small gifts to be hidden deep inside its arms.

Family was the key ingredient to our festivities. Our family celebrated then, and still today, on Christmas Eve. What a long day that was, waiting anxiously for everyone to arrive. I was the only grandchild to Nana and Grandpa Sawyer for nearly ten years, so to say that I was spoiled by them would be an understatement. I can see my grandfather with his arms full of beautifully decorated presents coming through the door with a smile on his face larger than any gift in his arms. Nana always went the extra mile to make the packages look so inviting. I especially loved, the sparkly tissue paper that she used, it was so pretty and sometimes you could peek through it. This is probably one reason that I tend to over indulge my grandchildren with specially wrapped gifts. Grandpa and Grammy

Atwood, always had animals to feed and cows to milk before they could come. "Will they ever get here?" Uncle Caleb and his family, would also join us after the farm chores were done. They had four children, thus with the birth of my sister, giving my Atwood grandparents six grandchildren, and in later years after my uncle's second marriage to Joyce (Robinson) and another four children: Benjamin, Matthew, Christopher, and Ryan; they now had a grand total of ten grandchildren. Therefore, they were not as indulgent with gifts, but it never mattered, their gifts were just as precious as the others. They too, were given in great love and in the joy of the season. Gifts from my parents were also small in number, but large in meaning. I knew that what I received was given with some sacrifice on their part. In 1969, during my teen years, they told me that there would be only one gift that year and to choose carefully. I wanted a "Three Dog Night Live at the Forum" album, SO BADLY! Back then, they were pretty expensive, even in today's standards. My mother cleverly hid the album inside a large box; it wasn't a sure thing until the wrapping paper was torn off and the gift was opened. Some of the other gifts that I received over the years, that might jog your memory are Barbie's doll companions; Ken, Midge, Alan, Skipper and Skooter. We wouldn't want Barbie to be lonely. Barbie's snazzy, peach-colored, Austin Healy sports car (easily seen through the tissue wrap), the Penny Brite doll, the three foot "Walk With Me" doll, and "Sister Belle Talking Doll" were all under the tree throughout the years. The walking doll did not, survive my sister's not so gentle play, but the talking doll with it's red cloth body, covered by the unique dress and its yellow yarn ponytail managed to remain intact. Even though I realize, that I am a part of today's problem with over indulgence, I also reflect on the commercialism of today. There were one or two highly advertised toys on the must have list in those years and not the mega choices of today, which now elicits the belief in the minds of the young that-- "I want everything in the toy store." That is, if you can find a toy store. Searching the Internet is not as much fun. Please bring back Claremont's magnificent Toy Castle. I played with my toys for years, as did my children. Not today, the playrooms and bedrooms are routinely cleansed of the "outgrown" and "the phase is over" toys, to make room for the influx of the new. How many versions of Barbie can there really be?

Santa always came to visit the believers. When we first lived in the small trailer, the hooves of his reindeer would clamor on the metal roof to alert us of his arrival. He entered the door with a booming "HO HO HO, Merry Christmas," asking if I had been a good little girl. Being the center of attention in these early years, I would sit on his lap and extol my charms. Santa would assure me that he would return to bring me gifts and fill my stocking, while I was sleeping "all tucked up in my bed, while dreams of sugarplums danced in my head." Where was Grandpa Sawyer during these visits from Santa? "You missed Santa, Grandpa!" As the number of children grew and we moved into the house, the traditional visit continued for all of the kids, and the eyes of the believers shone eagerly.

After all the presents were opened with squeals of delight, and everyone's thank-you for the gifts were all spoken, we sat down to share a big meal. Nana Sawyer, was famous for her spaghetti and meatballs served with hot homemade rolls, so this was often the requested fare. As my cooking skills progressed, my barbecued spareribs added a second choice to be ordered for the special meal. The evening was always topped off with great desserts prepared by Grammy Atwood and Aunt Becky, who were also great cooks. For the first Christmas in our new home, we were living in the basement, while the house was being completed. I can see my aunt as she descended the rough cellar stairway with a beautifully iced cake in her hands. She lost her balance slightly and her work of art went tumbling to the cellar floor. Oh My! Such a waste. Gram made the very best cake from graham crackers and chocolate whipped cream. It was melt in your mouth good! Luckily, we still had one cake left to eat.

The final tradition of the evening, before everyone departed for home, was the "lighting" of the Sawyer bulb. My grandfather Sawyer's family, purchased one of the first electric Christmas light sets sold in the early1900's. Throughout the years, we have kept a special set of lights and an original bulb. The bulb is fat and pointed near the top with a delicate tip, there are still a few specks of red paint remaining on it. This bulb is carefully lit each Christmas Eve, for a few seconds, long enough to see its dim light. This tradition began during my father's youth and now nearly a century later that bulb still lights up the hearts of our family, as we eagerly await its dim but persistent light for those few seconds. May it burn on for generations to come.

After all of the festivities had ended, dishes done, and wrappings cleared, it was time to set out the cookies and milk for Santa's return. I always hoped to sneak a peek at the old guy, but exhaustion took over and I would always miss him "Kissing Momma under the Mistletoe" and "filling our stockings all hung with care."

The next morning, Santa's gift was under the tree and my stocking was full, just like he had promised. He must have overlooked one or two of my "being naughty" moments. The stockings were filled with fruit, gum, Cracker Jacks complete with its hidden prize, a big book filled with rolls of lifesavers, and the essentials of life: a toothbrush, socks, undies, etc. What a great guy, bringing us things we need. He really does see everything.

One might think that Christmas would be over now. No Way! Christmas morning we packed up the car, Grandpa and Nana Sawyer also came, and we headed for the farm in Westminster,

Vermont, where my Atwood grandparents and Uncle Caleb's family lived. Once the cows were milked and the animals fed, we would share in another family celebration, which also included my aunt's family. This all bears a little explaining. On Christmas Eve, when my cousins came to our home, each member of their family received one gift from us and the same held true on our visit to their tree, we each received one gift from them. You might wonder, that as young children, if there was jealousy on our parts while the "home" children had multiple gifts to open, but truly I never felt left out or envious and I hope my cousins shared in this outlook. After the gifts, we were treated to a big breakfast, complete with fresh meat, eggs, and milk from the farm.

It wasn't over yet. In the afternoon, we would go to my grandparent's home. At first, they lived on one level of the farmhouse. In later years, when they sold their share of the farm to Caleb's family, they moved to a house just down the road from the farm. We would enjoy another tree in their home, where we would receive gifts of homemade mittens or slippers lovingly knit by Gram. This was a treasured moment, that my children and their young cousins also shared together in later years. The day was ended once again, with the family gathered around the table indulging in the fruits of my grandmother's labors. While the children played and the women cleaned up, the men would be napping, while the cows were awaiting their evening milking. Farm life doesn't stop, even for the magic of Christmas.

Spoiled Rotten

Little Miss Viola, was well known for being more than a slightly bit spoiled. She was also quite head strong when she had something of importance on her mind. Being the only child and the only grandchild on her paternal side for ten years, she had a pretty captive audience to express her desires to.

There was a little frog pond, a short distance from my house. I had to pass by this pond in order to go to the village; to go to school, stop by the store, visit a friend's house or whatever was on the other side of that pond that I wanted to do. A large snapping turtle had been hit by a car and sat decaying on the side of the road for days. Being summertime, passing by Mr. Snapper was not pleasant, but an alternative route to the village was a long way around. I don't recall exactly what specific concerns I had, but I did not want to go past that dead, scary carcass. How long does it take for a turtle of that size to rot away? As luck would have it, Grandpa and Nana Sawyer came for a visit and as always Grandpa understood the situation fully. My dear grandpa, put that nasty, old, dead, maggot-filled Mr. Snapper into the trunk of his new, well-maintained car and carted it off to parts unknown. Phew! My life in the village could continue; however, my grandparents' car sported a strange odor for a long time.

Grandpa Sawyer, was an avid sportsman in his day and he loved to ski. So naturally, he was sure that his sweet little Viola would also love this sport. I'm not sure exactly how old I was, but quite young, maybe five or six years old, when my grandparents gave me a whole ski package for Christmas. I received a ski outfit that would lighten up any fashion runway, new skis and boots, and a seasons pass to Mt. Tom Ski Area in Woodstock, Vermont. I was excited and nervous all in one package, but nothing could compete with the excitement that my grandpa was feeling. He smiled with pride as he sat me on that Poma Lift and watched me ride to the top with my skis gliding along in the packed down snow-path of those before me. As I approached the top, I was thinking, how do I get off this thing. Just as I rounded the corner and was headed back down, I started screaming for help. Some nice man pulled me to safety before I went face first down the hill on the lift. At this point, I'm crying! Let me rephrase that, I'm hysterical and I am not skiing down that MOUNTAIN! My loving, and fortunately fit grandpa, came to my aid, walked up the slope, and held my hand as I "skied" down the popular Mt. Tom for the first and last time. I sure hope they didn't spend too much money on that ski package. I still looked cute playing in the snow in my new snow outfit while standing on level ground. I did go on to be a pretty good athlete and make my grandpa proud, but my need for speed did not include doing so with two narrow pieces of wood on my feet. I did a little skiing in my teen years at Mt. Ascutney and Whaleback Mountain, however I never purchased any season passes. Recently, I drove by Mt. Tom, now designated by a historical marker for being the hill (Gilbert's) with the first ski tow in the United States. Guess what? It's really quite a small hill. Funny how time makes things look a little different.

Saturday, was dump day, the designated day to take the trash to the town dump. I believe that it was the only day that it was open. The old town dump was a social spot in town for the men to gather, to shoot the "bull" or the numerous rats that were scurrying amongst their banquet table of discarded food items in the dump. I used to like to go on this weekly jaunt with my father. Somehow, on one particular Saturday morning shortly after Halloween, my dad forgot how much that I cherished things that belonged to me. I was immediately stunned, when I saw my father toss my artfully carved Jack-O-Lantern over the steep, garbage filled bank. I could not believe my eyes, when my dear Mr. Pumpkin went tumbling down, bumping and bruising as it rolled to the bottom. How could he possibly throw MY pumpkin away? The tears flowed and the sobbing was inconsolable. My father choose the path of least resistance and worked his way to the bottom of the garbage heap and rescued my prized pumpkin. I smiled all the way home with my cherished rotten pumpkin sitting on my lap.

Many Walks of Life

I often think of cities as having all walks of life occupying their blocks and Burroughs. People who come together to live closely among others, but in many cases, to also lead very private lives amongst the hustle and bustle of city life.

Plainfield was also the home to people of many different walks of life during the years of my youth. Certainly those we called the city people that were members of the Cornish Colony, who came to live and summer among the townspeople, had a lifestyle that was unlike those who had lived and worked in our quaint river valley town their whole lives. Even those who had always made this area their home, came from different social and financial circumstances which led them on varied paths of making a living and providing homes for their families. Some of these homes were handed down through many generations, others were built by hand on newly acquired land, and there were those that were hastily put together to provide necessary, but inexpensive shelter. Unlike, some cookie cutter villages, where the homes all look similar, except for perhaps having an alternate color painted on the exterior, our town's homes were as varied as those who lived there.

My memory takes me back to the days when I loved traveling about on the back of my trusty horse. I can see the familiar homes with most of their occupants known to me, and I to them. Whether I was on the back roads of the countryside where homes could be miles apart or walking through the main village with its side roads reaching out to the more rural areas, my memory recalls studying the many different types of homes. Large old farmhouses sat on plots of farmland sprawling over acres of open fields that were surrounded by vast woodlands, while other farmhouses sat neatly on a small lot in the village. Tiny cottage style homes filled in the spaces between large two-story homes and could also be found hidden amongst the trees and shrubs lining the dirt roads in the country. I would also see, smaller crudely built homes with an elderly person living comfortably alone. In other cases, they were providing shelter for a large family with many children living in the cramped, but homey quarters. Like my family in the early years, some lived in simple trailers (now called mobile homes) and then in the 1960's, small inexpensive houses with what was considered a more modern style were being erected. They were very plain in their style, but might offer such things as block-masonry basements and electric baseboard heat, as opposed to dirt cellars and wood stoves. The bathrooms in the new homes were more up-to-date with built-in bathtubs with showers, instead of the old claw-footed tubs.

Sitting amongst the varied homes of the families fortunate enough to live in this very special place were beautiful estates and formal homes with gorgeous gardens and magnificent grounds. They could be found in or near the village, or laying on vast tracts of land in the countryside adding to the landscape of this beautiful river valley. These were mainly the homes and summer residences of members of the Cornish Colony, where the local people were able to find employment by helping to maintain these grand places.

In the late 1950's and early 1960's, my mother, was lucky to have been one of those employed by members of the Cornish Colony. She worked as a housekeeper for the Platts, the Littell-Palmer home, the Salingers, and the Saint-Gaudens Memorial, as it was called before it became a national historic site. Charles Platt, was the president of the board of trustees of the Memorial. His daughter, Clarissa

Platt Palmer, was the curator of Saint-Gaudens. She lived with her husband, Roger, and their two sons William and Thomas, in Aspet, the former home of the sculptor Augustus Saint-Gaudens. During the summer months, the first floor of Aspet, the studios once used by the great artist, his sculptures, and the grounds to include the reflecting pool were open to public tours. It is a beautiful site with amazing views of the Connecticut River Valley, with Mt. Ascutney providing the backdrop and completing the picture. It surprises me how many people from the area, have not yet found this magnificent treasure.

Little Miss Viola, was happy to be allowed to tag along, on Mom's work days. These beautiful homes, with their ornately decorated rooms filled with fine art and furnishings were a sight to see. So many unique and delightful objects for young eyes to take in. The outside was just as well designed as the interiors, some with piazzas or other outdoor sitting areas to view all of the glorious surroundings. The grounds were all beautifully landscaped, offering lush, colorful gardens filled with flowers and meticulously pruned hedgerows. The Cornish Colony flower gardens famously received national exposure through magazine coverage during that era. Many of these homes also had recreational areas such as in-ground pools and tennis courts for their families and guests to enjoy. The Platt home had a small studio on the grounds, where visiting artists could work. The Littell home had an added feature that I was always eager to use, an elevator. This memory reminds me of the old movie scenes showing an elevator's sliding gate door and the lever used to operate it. I hoped that Alfred Hitchcock wouldn't show up. "Mom, can I ride it, Please?"

The very best of times while accompanying my mother on her work days were spent at Saint-Gaudens. There was so much to explore and most often there was a group of us kids to make it more adventurous. My dear friend, Peggy Salinger and Clarissa's son, William Palmer, who were both kindergarten classmates of mine, also William's brother, Thomas, and I, never needed to look for things to occupy our hours. So many ideas, so little time. Hot summer days led us to the reflecting pool, with the beautiful goldfish lazily swimming about, and the gold colored statute turtles overseeing each end, while they spewed water through their mouths into the pool. I use the word pool here, because that is how it is described, however, in our eyes it really did seem like an Olympic sized pool. We swam in it, sometimes clothed and sometimes not. In reality, it is a small body of water not meant for swimming by anything, but the fish. We were often informed of this by all concerned, my mother, William's mother and the caretaker. A sweet, elderly, Swedish couple, Alan and Anna Jansson, were the caretakers of the property. They lived on site, in a small cottage, that sat hidden by high hedgerows, located near the ice house and livery stable. Their job was no small task considering the grand expanse of the property and the number of buildings to be cared for.

The Little Studio, was another place that playing in was frowned upon, but the cathedral ceiling of the main room was a great place for trying out echoing sounds. This intriguing space was lit by high windows, yet at the same time it was dark and cool, and simply full of mystery. The nude, arrowed statute of Diana watching over us only added to the excitement. The other rooms, which I think were the office and work areas of the great sculptor were also interesting to the curious mind. "Remember! Do Not Touch Anything!"

Hidden sculptures sat among the gardens and groomed hedges which provided a perfect setting for playing, hiding in, and getting into poison ivy. Not to worry, we could always cool off its itch in the reflecting pool. Thank you William, for introducing Peggy and me to that "wondrous" plant. Can you really get poison ivy in all of those places? Yes!

Inside days, found us climbing the long winding service staircase leading from the kitchen to the third floor which were once the servant's quarters. With wild imaginations we played house in these rooms. Although, this area was smaller and simpler than the other floors of Aspet, it was brightly lit by the warm summer sun shining through the paned windows with their panoramic views fit for a king. I hope the servants once living there enjoyed this area as much as I did.

Despite the many walks of life arising from the varied backgrounds and lifestyles of the people living in our not-so-small-time town, they came together as one. While maintaining their individual privacy, the people of our wonderful town lived as neighbors, and built a village community that met the needs of the whole and especially the lucky youth growing up there, like myself.

Plainfield Families

As the styles of homes differed, so did the types of families, living in the community. Each family had qualities that were vital to the health of the village life, in which they were helping to nurture, in conjunction with others. I believe, that most families have strengths and weaknesses that are the foundation upon which they live their daily lives. My family was no different. My parents were not financially well off and like many families during this time, they found life to be difficult. My mother needed to work outside of the home and at times my father's illnesses did not allow him to hold a job. Even though I led a simple life, it was not always problem free. Adult stress was something that I learned to cope with at an early age. I found many avenues of escape from the day to day problems of life. Besides my times of glorious freedoms, I was also, most blessed to have been able to share in the lives of some very special families. These families touched my life and shared their wealth of family love. Their values had an immeasurable influence on me and who I was to become. They were a beacon calling out to me, an only child for nearly ten years, come and take part in what we have to offer. I could probably write an encyclopedia on the countless families of Plainfield, all of whom were important and influential during my youth. However, due to the limit of time and pages, I'm going to focus on a few families who had a significant impact on my family and me, in an era that was so different from many of the social connections in today's time.

Although, it might seem insignificant to the reader who is not familiar with Plainfield, or even other rural country towns, you might wonder why I mention road names and identify other areas by the name associated to them. Many of Plainfield's roads are named after families who once lived there, and in some cases they were named for particular crops grown in that area or the nature of the landscape. Also important to understand, is that many of these areas represented a village in those days. Village in this sense means just a few homes, unlike the Village of Plainfield, with its community buildings and stores. Nonetheless, each small village's importance is a vital part to the story.

The community as a whole, but in particular these families played a very important role in my life, growing up in a not-so-small-time town, called Plainfield.

◇◇◇◇

The Jordan farm has belonged to a member of the Jordan family for well over a hundred years, and continues today, to be occupied by the sixth generation of Jordans. The farm sits at the top of a very large, steep glacier formed hill. The farmhouse, its land and buildings surround the intersection of where Westgate Road meets Spencer and Kenyon Roads, creating the perfect setting for families and their children to come from all directions and villages to share with the Jordan family. Although, this farm is no longer operated as a dairy farm, while I was growing up, it ran smoothly under the reins of Bill, Alice, and Bill's brother, lovingly known to everyone as Uncle Ray. They raised a large herd of Holstein and Jersey cattle. Bill and Alice's children, Robert, Donald and Deborah, like all farm kids, played a critical role in the daily operation of the farm. The family also raised a host of other farm animals typical to old New England farms, such as pigs and chickens. Crops of corn were grown to feed their cattle and they gathered hay, both on the farm and by arrangement on various other local fields. Uncle Ray's vegetable garden, which was beyond comparison, fed the Jordan family and supplemented many of the neighbors' tables. As if all of this was not enough to fill the hours of their days, Bill drove school bus and Alice nurtured the youth with her many skills as our 4-H Leader.

    The Jordan children and I, played in the fields, the barns, the pond, the woods, their yard, and in their house. When other children joined us, they would travel from their homes using the three intersecting roads. The Meyettes and the Barretts came by Kenyon Road. Kids from the Village of Plainfield, along with those living on it, used Westgate. Spencer Road was the chosen path for the Mill Village bunch, where among others the Buster Wilder family lived. Little villages of youngsters all meeting in one big happy place, on top of that hill.

    I learned so many skills from Alice Jordan over the years. She was a 4-H leader for more than two decades. Our club was called "The Happy Homemakers." I spent many hours in her kitchen cooking from recipes, preparing meals, and preserving vegetables from the garden. I also learned candle making, studied babysitting, photography, citizenship and gained horsemanship skills, that I could carry over into the barn. My favorite lessons revolved around sewing. There was nothing that Alice couldn't teach you about this art, she had the skills and patience to fix the many mistakes made by me and countless others. I can still feel the treadle of her old Singer sewing machine, under my feet, and hear the purr of the bobbin shuttle passing to and fro. I hadn't sewn in about thirty years, since my children were young. However, in recent years I decided to start sewing again and all of the lessons came streaming back to me. I was able to make some special items for my grandchildren to cherish, such as their first quilts and Halloween costumes. Though, I do not profess to be a master seamstress, I found the love that I put into them, more than made up for the crooked seams.

The neighbors, my family included, loved to gather at the Jordan home for their "get-togethers," sometimes planned and sometimes spur of the moment. As I mentioned earlier, a great spot for water fun was at their pond where we also enjoyed picnics and barbecues. Families would gather to have cookouts and rousing neighborhood baseball games on their back lawn. Uncle Ray was quick to remind us, not to hit the ball into his garden.

During the cold weather months, Alice's kitchen always smelled of hot cider, donuts, sugar on snow, or whatever delicacy she came up with after a hayride, or sliding party. Fall hayrides were a favorite of all, young and old, even if it did include plenty of chaffing and itching from the hay. We would ride in a wagon full of hay and look up at the beautiful night sky, filled with dancing stars and the cold fall moon. Couples would hug each other to keep warm and steal a kiss or two. The sounds of singing and laughter on those chilly nights still ring loudly and fondly in my ears.

My family owned a traverse sled. The vision of this sled remains in my mind and I can feel it under me, like I was just sliding on it yesterday. I have always known that they were not common, so I decided to do a little research on it and found that it is, a true rarity, which makes it even more special in my eyes today. Every winter, the families on the hill would don their winter gear and head to the Jordan's on a weekend night, after a good heavy snowstorm, and the roads had been freshly plowed, but not yet sanded. My dad would hook up the sled to our car and up the steep climb to Jordan farm we would go. When everyone arrived, the first lucky group would load up the sled and get ready for the adventure. The sled's long, slender wooden body sat higher than a regular sled and was held up by three movable sections with runners on them. You sat with your feet up on rail sections that ran along the sides and were positioned slightly lower than the seat. About a dozen people could fit on the long, plank seat keeping their bodies tucked low and close to prevent any wind resistance. The more the merrier and the faster we would go on the thrilling descent of the glacier carved mountainside with its sharp declines, short flat spots, and all of the twists and turns offered on an exciting roller coaster ride. Heading down the lengthy trail, we would go with lightning speed. One of the men, usually my dad, would steer the sled with their feet from the front seat. The snow-covered dirt road was no obstacle to the giant sled once it picked up speed. We'd cross with hopeful accuracy, over the narrow bridge spanning the Blow-Me-Down Brook by our house and then during the final leg of the ride we would ascend up a short, curved knoll until with luck we would reach well down, about two hundred yards or so, onto the flats of Westgate Road. The ride took us about a mile from where we had started. I wish I could remember the furthest spot that we ever managed to reach. I believe it was somewhere near the Adams and Morse homes. Uncle Ray would wait on the flats for us to arrive and he would stop any cars that might be traveling in our direction. Although the road was not heavily traveled, if a car did come along, they waited happily for our ride to end. Can you imagine people being that patient today? "What do you mean I have to wait here for a sled coming down the road?" After the ride was over, we would hop in the farm wagon hitched to the back of Uncle Ray's great little jeep and head back up the hill, sled in tow, so that we could do it all over again. I was so sad, when years later I found that beautiful giant rotting behind my parent's barn.

The Jordans, as well as being neighbors, friends, and leaders, were also my employers for many summers. I owned horses which was a lot of fun, but also expensive, with feed being at the top of the pricey list. So, during my teen years, I worked the long, hot summers in the hay fields alongside the Jordan children, Bill, and Uncle Ray to earn hay, which would feed my horses during the winter. I became a pretty good hay stacker atop the wagon, able to build a high and stable load of bales that would withstand the sometimes long trip back to the barn. Some of the fields were on their property and some were many miles away. Needless to say, in those days there was no need to visit the gym. While working in the hot fields, we would drink cool water that we transported in milk cans, using a metal ladle, and if we were far from the farm, Alice would pack us a lunch. There was one field in particular that I dreaded with each upcoming harvest. This field was located at the corner of Thrasher Road and Route 12-A. It was riddled with snakes, my biggest fear. Anyone who has worked in a hay field knows that snakes get caught up along with the hay in the baler. Dead or alive, when those bales of hay were tossed up to me with a snake hanging out, I was out of there. The story goes, that my feet never hit the ground until I was a long distance from the wagon. If they didn't want to lose their stacker, they would take care of those slithering creatures before tossing the bale.

As is so often true in life, spur of the moment adventures are sometimes the very best. One beautiful, hot, summer day, the Sawyers and the Jordans, decided to take an unplanned day trip to the Townsend Dam in Vermont, for a day of swimming and picnicking. So, the women gathered up the food, the kids collected the beach toys, and the men were tasked with how we were going to fit ten people in my parents old Ford Econoline van. There were four Sawyers and the six Jordans. Those vans allowed two in the front, although I think my baby sister Carol sat on Mom's lap. (Remember it was long before seat belt requirements.) A wicker patio bench seat was added to accommodate the other adults and the rest of kids squeezed in amongst the food, towels, and toys. We have laughed many times about the "Plainfield Beverly Hillbillies," headed off the mountain. What a wonderful day it was! In revisiting this very special day, I am drawn to the realization, that the most important part of this story was that Uncle Ray went with us. Although the eyes of us children, saw differences in others and questions were on the tips of our tongues, they were but curious questions of youth and not the judgements held by many during this time in society. In his early teen years, Uncle Ray, developed a growth that caused a visible deformity to his skull and affected an eye. People with afflictions, as they were called in those days, were often closeted off-- meaning, not included by their families and there was little to no discussion of the "problem." The Bill Jordan home, never secluded Uncle Ray from any event held on the farm and to everyone who dearly loved him he was just Uncle Ray. Even though, our eyes might have seen the differences, our minds did not. Sadly, I am told that the years of his youth, before living with Bill's family, were ones of seclusion. He therefore, rarely felt comfortable enough to leave the farm for any social events. Yet, on this day, he chose to take this trip with us and his enjoyment alone, made the day priceless. It warms my heart to think that he felt safe amongst his family and friends enjoying the day from the protection of the wooded picnic area, alongside the dam's beach waterfront.

The last Jordan adventure, that I will share, is that of maple sugaring. The Jordan's sugarhouse was located on the section of their property bordering Spencer Road. Weekdays, during sugaring season, I would get off at their school bus stop with the Jordan kids, just to go to the sugarhouse. Even though, it made my trip home about a mile longer and that Spencer Road was a long, steep hill climb, I didn't care. I wanted to go to the sugarhouse and "help" gather the sap. I'm not sure, Bill and Uncle Ray always found us kids to be extremely helpful. The sap was collected from the old metal buckets, the old-fashioned way. This meant hauling buckets filled with sap through waist deep snow back to the sugarhouse, sitting nestled in the woods. The warmth of the sugarhouse was always so inviting. I will never forget, the sweet smell of sap boiling and the beautiful amber color of the finest maple syrup when it was ready to be drawn off the boiler. I can still see Uncle Ray threading the temperature ready syrup from a large metal spoon until it ran in a perfect thread-like flow, eyeing it to see if it was ready to be poured into the tin cans. If we were lucky, and often we were, when we arrived at the farmhouse, Alice would treat us to sugar on snow; this treat consisted of a bowl of icy, cold snow with hot maple syrup drizzled over it. The syrup worked its way through the snow into a lacy covering, which would harden into a delicious candy. While gathering the snow for this, we would joke about watching out for any yellow snow left behind by the roaming animals. Being in the sugarhouse was one of the highlights of early spring. I hope that my grandchildren will experience the art of maple sugaring, at least once while they are young.

◇◇◇◇

The MacLeay family lived at the bottom of the hill below the Jordan farm in a small house surrounded by the woodlands. The MacLeays, Don, Vera, Scott and Danny, were a very large and important part of my life while I was growing up. Their warm, cozy home was always open to me, where I spent many, many hours eating Vera's bountiful treats and playing. Scotty, Danny and I played in the woods by the hours, especially in the little cabin hidden in the trees, which sat on the bank near their house. It was a plain cabin with limited furniture; kind of fort like. The outside was painted green and had a small porch at the entryway. Don and Scott recently shared with me that this cabin had previously been used as a ground observation tower to monitor and report small aircraft activity to the Albany Air Force Center. These observation activities were done by a citizen volunteer group. This program was started by the U. S. Air Force out of concern for aircraft that could fly below the radar system during the Korean War. After it was no longer in use, Don had it moved to their property in the mid 1950's. Its original location was just below my home, on a little side trail by the frog pond in the hollow, which lead to the top of a knoll.

Don was an avid pilot, and it was always a treat to go flying with him in his Super Cub. There was no radio or radar. All the flying was done visually with limited instrumentation. If one remembers, he also drove like he was flying. There was a tale that was told for years by the locals. He was stopped for speeding and the police officer said, "Hey Buddy, can I see your pilot's license?" Don obliged him by pulling his pilot license out. After a bewildered look, and a little chuckle the officer let him go. "No Ticket!"

Another of Don's talents, was playing the steel guitar. He joined with other men from the area to play in a country dance band called, "Woody and the Ramblers." They would travel to different venues on weekends to entertain at local square dances. Vera almost always included us kids in these evenings, we sure did love to dance. I still enjoy hearing the calls, such as four hands square, do sa do, allemande left, and promenade. Sounds no longer heard very often these days. What fun it was to dance to the "Virginia Reel," the "Bunny Hop" and the "Mexican Hat Dance."

Winter fun always included sledding parties. Don would make sure the neighborhood kids had the perfect setting for a night of fun. He lit up the large, snow-covered knoll in the field across from their home with generator powered lighting. It was the ideal place to glide over the snow packed and sometimes ice covered surface on our Red Flyers of all sizes, those fast and furious metal flying saucers, and the all-time favorite wooden toboggan which was loaded with as many of us as it could possibly fit. There were also skiers among us, some better than others. I definitely fit into the later category. My first pair of skis, were a short wooden set that you put on by just slipping your boots into a canvas strap. My parents used old jar rubbers to hold my skis onto my feet. Then I graduated, to a very long, skinny wooden pair, with pointed tips that curled up at the end into some sort of ball shape decorating the tip; they also had a canvas strap to just slip your feet into. The more modern version came with a metal foot piece that your feet stepped into. They were held on with a metal strap fitting around your heel and then you pulled the metal lever forward to secure your foot. The accompanying ski poles had the round bottom metal ring that was held on by leather straps. We made all of these snow gliders even speedier by rubbing wax bars on their bottoms and runners. I wonder how many boxes of that wax we went through? Those glorious winter evenings, all ended with wet clothes, frozen toes, fingers, and noses; which were all soothed by generous amounts of treats and hot chocolate with mounds of marshmallow.

Another favorite pastime, was the biggest and best trampoline known to mankind, at least that's what we were sure of. The "cool" trick was to bounce each other off onto the ground, the higher you went the better luck you had at this. I still have a slight knot on the back of my head from a visit with the metal rail. I could actually put my finger in the hole in my head when it happened. YUK!! Did I ever share that tidbit with my parents? I recently visited Scott and his family. He had his home built in the field across from his original family home, where Don once again lives. Imagine my delight when I saw in his backyard, a trampoline now enjoyed by his son and friends. The circle of childhood life in Plainfield continues.

I was also surprised to learn from Scott during this visit, that the land on which Scott's home sits, has been in their family dating back to the original land grant deeded by King George the Third and Governor Benning Wentworth, in 1761. The Westgate Road name comes from Scott's ancestors.

Gramma Bessie (Westgate) Hill, Vera MacLeay's mother, lived in the house in the middle of the hill leading to the Jordan farm. I could see her house from mine, as it sat nestled in the mountainside between Westgate and Dodge Roads. She loved to have her grandsons, Scotty and Danny, and me, visit with her. She was a loving grandmother to all. Her kind and smiling face will be ever present to me.

In 1962, the MacLeay family along with their Gramma Bessie, moved to the grand home on Route 12-A, formerly known as the Kingsbury Tavern built in 1802, in the village of Plainfield. The large-man pond, earlier shared with you sat on this property. Their home having been a tavern also offered big spacious rooms to play in, including one upstairs, which was formerly the ballroom. It was a vast dance hall with wooden benches lining the walls of the room. I'm sure that in years past, the seats were filled with eager dancers tapping their feet to the music filling the air. We loved to pretend that we were attending a grand ball and danced our hearts out.

When the great outdoors beckoned for us to play outside, there was a neat arbor covering the walkway and a big barn in the backyard to play in, but my favorite spot sitting next to the adjacent cemetery, was the little "teahouse." It was, and still is today, a small potting shed, painted white, with paned windows complete with window boxes and shutters. In my mind, it was truly the replica of a small cottage that you might find hidden in the forest in some fairy tale. Danny and I, sometimes joined by others, especially loved to hang out there by the hours and let our imaginations take over.

Unlike today, we had only a handful of toys to play with, so we created our own by using plant pots, old glass jars, and discarded furniture from the barn including old wooden boxes, that we used to make our table setting and stove from. We also improvised with odds and ends of dishes, pots and pans no longer in household use, pinecones, leaves, and stones for food, and whatever else we could get our hands on. Tree branches were great brooms and we decorated our playhouse with wildflowers. We could have been having a tea party, playing house, or pretending to be going to school; it didn't matter, life was good. I wonder if children today have as much fun with all of their plastic toys, which require little imagination.

My connection with the MacLeay family, continued into my college years. Scott transported my roommate Mary-Jo Barto and me, back and forth to college at UNH in Durham. Like his father Don, Scott too must have held a pilot's license, as his great, little, yellow VW Bug would fly at great speeds down the highway. Scott enjoyed his radio, and even more, he liked to adjust the dial almost continuously during the entire trip, while somehow he still managed to keep the VW between the lines at warp speed. He lived in the Alexander Hall dormitory, where we played rousing games of Ping Pong. His hall was right across the narrow street from our dorm, Hetzel Hall. One winter, we built snow forts and had hard-fought snowball fights. Once, I think, the girls must have won, because that night our room's ground floor windows were packed with snow between the glass and the security screens. They were packed so tightly that we could not see out of them for weeks. Scott and I, also spent many hours on the snowmobile trails exploring the woods of Plainfield and Cornish.

As an adult, Dan's career took him from the area. Years later, when he was back home visiting, we had a wonderful reunion at my home in Claremont over dinner. I hope we'll have that opportunity again, some day soon.

◇◇◇◇

When Gramma Bessie Hill went to live with the MacLeays, her former home, once again, was filled with life by the LaPan family, complete with a new friend for me, Jean. Gordon LaPan and his wife "Timmy" had four children: Nancy, Jean, Dan, and Joan. At about eight years old, Jean and I became fast friends, a relationship that has survived our adult years of rearing children, family obligations, careers and in general, life's craziness; which sadly has made little time to spend with each other, during those later years.

As kids, we did nearly everything that kids do together, spending countless hours in each other's homes, including sleepovers. On warm summer nights we would sleep out, beneath the brilliant stars twinkling above. A night sky in the country, is unlike any other; there are no man-made lights to interfere with the beauty of the scene above you. When we were lucky, we would see a falling star as its life was burning out, and of course, we would always make our wish upon the falling ball of fire. The hunt was always on to find the Big Dipper constellation and its counterpart the Little Dipper. The Milky Way, was sometimes clearly seen with its many stars and swirls of wispy cloud-like markings spreading widely across the dark sky, adding its own mystique to the vast night expanse. In addition to the twinkling stars, the moon would be shining in its current phase, sometimes a full moon or perhaps a mere crescent. Whatever its phase, it always offered curiosity to an imaginative child. Was there really a man in the moon? Is it really made of cheese? Another very special light show, that we enjoyed during those lazy summer nights were the lightning bugs, known to some as fireflies. They would light up the fields in countless numbers, providing us with a beautiful display of fireworks. We loved to chase and catch them in old glass jars, as they tried to elude us by turning on and off their lights--like when your parents flickered the porch light, to call you in for the night. Where have all of the fireflies gone, I rarely see them anymore.

When I discovered that Jean also loved Barbie, our friendship was cemented. Jean's Mother, had many talents, one of which, was that she was an excellent seamstress. She made a lot of our doll clothes, many of them matching, so that our dolls could dress alike. I still have my Barbie dolls and many of their accessories; thankfully they survived my sister's not so gentle play days. My daughter enjoyed them as well, and she added to the collection. Now, I anxiously await my granddaughter's interest in them, so I can play Barbies once again.

Mrs. LaPan also sewed beautiful clothes for her children. I remember being envious of the colorful and unique items that she made. One year in particular, she made winter jackets for them, and either my "green-eyed monster" showed its ugly head, or perhaps I begged, but she generously and lovingly made one for me. I felt like a winter princess, dressed warmly in that precious jacket.

When we couldn't think of anything "fun" to do, we played a little game of "guess what you are tasting now." We'd choose food items from the cupboards or fridge and put a teaspoon full of it, in the other's mouth. We would be blindfolded during the game to ensure no cheating. Whoever correctly guessed the most items was the winner. On one such taste testing event, Jean put a rather large sample of homemade horseradish in my mouth. I'm not sure if I ever played that "fun" game again.

Jean and I loved to play outdoors, just as much as we enjoyed our indoor time with Barbie and her friends. The field bordering our property, was part of the farm formerly owned by my grandparents,

Francis and May Atwood, and this field offered many places to play in: amongst the trees growing in the woods surrounding the field, in the tall grass, and especially in the streams that fed the Blow-Me-Down Brook. There was an old abandoned barn, which called to the adventurous to come play in. It had been many years since the barn had been fully used, so the falling down nature of it led to curious nooks and crannies, where discarded items hid, as well as it being the home to various wild animals. All of the strange sounds emitting from it could be a little spooky at times. This barn, was the stage, in a recurring dream (nightmare, really) that I had throughout my youth. Perhaps these dreams were penance for the following story. Each spring, Jean and I were under strict instructions to stay out of the streams, which ran rapid with cold spring water shedding down from the hills after the snow melt from the heavy winter storms. We had sailboats that did lively and exciting dances in those rushing waters; resisting this fun, was more than we could bear, even though we knew that we would eventually get wet. The stream's waters ran open in some spots, but there were also places where large sections of ice would hang out over the running water. We would race alongside the stream to watch our boats bob up and down, and in and out of the pools swirling between rocks. In places, the stream ran out in the open field and at other times it was hidden under stands of trees with their low hung branches covering the water. Downstream, we would wait anxiously for our boats to reappear. Occasionally, they would get caught on something and we've have to crawl our way under those umbrella-like branches to untangle our boats so that they could sail freely once again. One bright, spring day, after we were sternly reminded to stay away from the icy waters, we raced toward the stream which ran next to the old barn, to sail our prized vessels. There before my eyes, was a large, beautiful icy-blue shelf of ice hanging out and hovering over the stream. What a perfect spot for setting sail from. However on this day, while out on the ice of this forbidden stream, the ice gave way and I found myself--clothes, boots, and all--in the water. I will leave the rest to your imagination. Let's just say this was not the first, or last time that I was grounded.

Another one of our adventures that left my parents a little unhappy (there were probably many more) involved our old barn, which used to be a shed used for storing lime. It originally sat adjacent to the aforementioned vacant barn. My parents had it moved by a skidder to our property in the late 1950's, and it became a barn for my horses. The barn had an overhead storage area, which consisted of open beams with some boards to provide support for the stored items. My parents, had likely forgotten what was up there after the many years that had passed, but they decided that we girls should clean this area. In our minds, that meant taking down everything that was up there and no one had mentioned doing it in an organized fashion. Therefore, we proceeded to throw down every single item into the horse stalls below. This project required us to carefully study each item first, before discarding it. We had an exciting find, there was an old army duffle bag belonging to my father, which contained love letters that my parents had written to each other while he was serving in the Army. Needless to say, we felt obligated to read the many pages of juicy information and then toss them down, page by page, into the horse stalls with all of the other treasures we had found. After all, we were going to discard them anyways, so why bother to place them neatly back in their envelopes. Have I mentioned that one of my least favorite chores was to muck out the horse stalls? Therefore, it did not happen on a regular basis. Are you getting the picture? My parents must have decided that we were too quiet and that we had not been seen in a long time, so they came to check on our progress. The neighborhood was no longer quiet, and the rest of the job was no longer as exciting as it had been earlier.

Our delight in playing outdoors was not hampered by the weather. Our old fashioned northeast winters, were cold and snowy. We enjoyed sliding on the snow covered hills, skating across the frozen ice, making snow angels and building snowmen-- decorated with sticks for arms with the ends covered by mittens, a carrot nose, rocks for eyes and a mouth. It was further adorned with a corn cob pipe, a stocking cap and perhaps a scarf. We also had great fun building snow forts, that we used for protection from each other, or sometimes other kids who would join in with us, for a snowball fight. This was good practice, because one never knew when a rigorous snowball fight might erupt, as we traveled about town.

These practice sessions came in handy one sunny, winter afternoon. We had to walk home from the village after school. Mr. Bennett and his lovely wife, lived in the third house on the left on Westgate Road. Mrs. Bennett was always treating us kids to goodies and Mr. Bennett shared a wave, a friendly smile, and kind words with us while tending his large vegetable garden during the summer months, or clearing snow in the winter. On this day, as we passed by his house after school, he started pelting us with snowballs from behind his freshly built fort. Naturally, we felt obliged to accept his challenge and return fire. Wouldn't you know, that my father would be just turning the corner onto Westgate Road, at that very moment. He was a lot less than pleased, to see me pummeling Mr. Bennett with my perfectly formed snowballs. When my father was angry, which was not a rarity in those days, it was best to just sit back and go along for the ride. There was NO room for explaining. After a long ride home, a half of mile at the most, and a very stern lecture on respect for my elders, my father drove me back down the hill to the Bennett home. I was instructed, to make my proper apologies for my poor behavior. Mr. Bennett, feeling a little guilty himself for having started the earlier ruckus, explained the truth of the situation to my father, however I'm not sure the sport ever held as much of a thrill for me again.

◇◇◇◇

During our early teen years, Jean and I would have a new friend. In the mid 1960's, another very special family moved onto the hill. Ed and Joanne Martin bought the house right up the road from us, which bordered our next door neighbors, the Eatons. They, like the LaPans, had four children: Sherry, Kathy, Edward, and Scotty. Jo-Annie, as we lovingly called her, was the "mother" to all of us kids, she also served the youth as an assistant 4-H leader, and provided daycare for several children from the town. She had the ability to remain calm through almost any situation. Sherry was my age, and she soon joined the gang of friends living on the hill. We too, spent countless hours together playing and sharing each other's homes and meals.

Like most teens, music was a major part of my life, and my little 45rpm record player went everywhere with me, including to Sherry's house. It looked like a ladies cosmetic case of the time and could it ever play those tunes, scratchy sounds and all, with that "precision" needle tracking those grooves. I could kick myself for getting rid of that treasure, I've searched the Internet, with no luck. Once, while Sherry and I were playing in her room and listening to those irreplaceable vinyl records, I suddenly broke out with the chicken pox. I was so "freaked out" by what I was seeing on my already teenage acne riddled body. My new complexion was none too pretty, and the newly formed bumps, itched like crazy. In Jo-Annie's kind and loving way, she assured me that I would not look like this for the rest of my life. Of course, with so many children around, it became an "epidemic" and spread like wildfire. Not exactly the way to make friends, but after all we were always being told to share. I was happy to oblige and not be the only "freak" in town.

The girls from the hill, Jean, Sherry and I, were always looking for ways to be even more beautiful, so as teenagers we experimented with make-up and hair styles. I recall green and blue eye shadow that came in tubes like lipstick and an equally attractive white lip color. Oh My! I had very long, thick hair that we ironed, yes, with an iron on the ironing board, to ensure that it would be straight. During other times, when my mood or the in-vogue style changed, I would want it set in huge curling rollers. After which, it had to be dried in one of those portable hair dryers, with a hose attached to the hair bonnet, that was blowing hot, dry air. Still, it took forever to dry your hair. The price of being beautiful! Being true teenage girls, we also had to be in fashion with just the right shoes, I still love my shoes. Imelda Marcos watch out! Our pocketbooks were gigantically large and very colorful, as I write this, I see an advertisement sitting on the coffee table with familiar photos of such bags. Funny how the fashions, keep cycling back through. Recently, I bought my granddaughter a new outfit for her birthday. While shopping for it, I remarked to my husband, look the 60's are back. I was known for ripping and bleaching my new jeans before being seen in public. I wonder if I could now start a new craze and make some money? My peace belt still holds a place of honor in my drawer. How many times have we gone from minis to maxis over the years? My mini days are long over.

My baby sister, Carol, was about the same age as the Martin's youngest child, Scotty. While my parents worked, Carol spent many hours being cared for in the arms of Jo-Annie, who endearingly called her "Caca." This name followed my sister into adulthood. Only Jo-Annie could get away with something like this, as there was no question in anyone's mind of the love and commitment that she had for "her children."

Like all friends, Sherry and I had our ups and downs. One such moment was when Sherry asked me for my renowned, or so I thought, recipe for homemade whoopie pies, which I gladly gave her. A few hours later, she called me to say that if I hadn't wanted to give her the recipe, I should have just said so. I was confused about what she meant, but I was sure that she was hopping mad, after all, they were being baked for a special young man coming to dinner. I hurriedly went to her aid and found her lamenting over a very large cookie sheet holding one massive, chocolate mound, instead of the numerous small cookies that she had perfected. I quickly discovered, that she had written down six cups of shortening, instead of the intended six tablespoons. Together, we whipped up another batch and the friendship was saved, once again.

Joanne and my mother remained best friends throughout their lives, until her long, hard fight with cancer took Jo-Annie from us in 2009. It was a major loss, to all who knew her. Time and distance have kept Sherry and me apart, but we have managed to keep up some contact. Fortunately, we were able reach out to each other at the tough times in our lives. Once again, it proves that those early bonds made in our not-so-small-time town, remain important when times are difficult.

◇◇◇◇

Our next door neighbors were Bernard, known to all as "Shorty" and Mildred Eaton, who owned the beautifully manicured property across from our home. They were gentle and kind, and shared these qualities with the neighborhood children. Mrs. Eaton was always neat in her appearance with her hair in an impeccable bun. She looked like she was dressed for a trip to town even though she almost always wore dusters and aprons. Her persona reminds me of Aunt Bee on <u>Mayberry RFD,</u> but instead of hearing Bee's admonishing remark of "Now Andy!" It was Mrs. Eaton saying, "Now Bernie!" Mr. Eaton could be seen several times daily, backing his treasured car of the moment out of his garage attached to the big red barn, which sat at the end of the short drive. The barn seemed to tower over the small cottage style home. One such prized ride, was his bright yellow 1968 Dodge Charger, with all of the chrome attachments that an eye could hold. That car was surely the envy of all males, young and old, for miles around. We were sure that "Shorty" was going to rub the paint right off of it, he polished it so many times. He was also noted for his cigar smoking. That cigar would bob up and down in his mouth with every stroke of the wax cloth. We also wondered if Mrs. Eaton really needed that many things from the village store, because he certainly made a few trips up and down the hill--sporting that car. Good thing gas was much cheaper back then.

    Their tender and loving nature was expressed daily in the operation of their business, called "The Doggie Motel." They boarded the special canine members of many families in their kennel, trust me I have a hard time calling it that, because it was truly a motel for dogs. If you have ever been in a kennel, the smell is hard to forget, but I think you could have eaten off the floors of this fine establishment. Each pet had its own suite (pen), complete with a private exercise yard. They were well equipped with special beds, food and water trays, toys, and whatever else a special pet might want. Mr. Eaton spent a great deal of time and individual attention tending to their every need and desire. He even left a radio playing in the kennel at all times, adding to their contentment, rarely was there a barking dog. I'm sure that there were many grateful pet owners over the years. Some years later, the kennel housed the Humane Society. The noise level was somewhat different, as the barking was continuous, and annoying in the quiet country air.

Like most kids, my friends and I were looking to find ways to earn a few bucks. On hot summers days, we would set up a lemonade stand at the top of our property and just across from the Eaton's home. Traffic in those days was a little slow, therefore so was business. Westgate Road did not have a great deal of passing cars, so waiting for cars to pass by could take hours. Mr. Eaton must have felt sorry for us, because he was definitely our very best customer. I felt that in order for us to be successful, that we needed to have a nice presentation. My mother's beautiful cobalt blue, cut glass pitcher would be the perfect prop for gaining the attention of those passing motorists. I don't even have to tell you, but yes, we broke it. In earlier years, the road had been widened and it must have covered an old wooden water box on the side of the road. This box was once used to provide water for livestock that were traveling by. We discovered the old box on the edge of the road when we were searching for a place to bury the spoils of the broken pitcher. Although, the surface of the box was covered over, when we were at eye level with the road, we found a perfect opening on the side of the box in which to hide the broken pieces, completely out of sight. The old water box now holds several pieces of that pretty pitcher. "Does anyone know where my blue pitcher went?"

The Eaton's had two grandchildren, David and Debra, who spent a great amount of time with their grandparents over the years. David was older, and might I add, quite handsome. It was a treat to hang out with him and his friends on those rare occasions when girls were allowed. They were avid hunters and outdoorsman, and even tomboy me, did not live up to the manly standards set by the big boys. Every country teenage boy desires a cabin and David's grandfather, made his dream come true. It sat hidden in the woods, adjacent to the man-made pond that we swam and fished in, and during the winter months glided over the ice on. I can't recall how the inside of the cabin looked, except for just some basic furniture and perhaps a gun rack or two. The outside, however, remains vividly in my mind. It was painted the same dark red as the "motel," and it had animal pelts tacked onto the sides of the cabin, to display the great hunters' gaming conquests. Even today, when I see a red squirrel or hear their noisy, warning chatter, my mind wanders to the numerous medals of honor, that I saw so proudly and "grossly" attached to the side of that cabin.

Although Deb was about five years older than me, we shared many special times together over the years. In her teens, she generously let me hang out with her older friends, listen to all the popular 45rpm records and in general, engage in teenage girl talk. It was here, that I first heard the song "Louie, Louie." Remember how scandalous that song was then? If only we could be that "racy" now. Even with the difference in ages, we still enjoyed our many hours of playing house and dolls. She had the most beautiful dolls and doll furniture that my eyes had ever seen. The upstairs bedroom in the Eaton's cottage style home, was Deb's room. The closet storing her treasures ran under the eaves, it was a long and low, and each time the door opened, it was like entering a special toy world. I still have the cradle, that Mrs. Eaton (I hope with Deb's permission) gave me many years ago. This is the cradle that I spoke of earlier, that holds my special quilt and has since been lovingly used by my daughter, Tracey and now my granddaughter, Brooke. It is yet, another of my childhood treasures.

In the early 1970's, the Eatons moved to Florida. Mrs. Eaton continued to correspond with me until she passed in recent years at the age of 98. Deb opened Annie McCassar's Restaurant in Claremont, New Hampshire, in the late 1970's. This fine eatery had a wonderful atmosphere and great food. I celebrated my twenty-fifth birthday, sitting in the corner fan chair, being treated like a queen.

◇◇◇◇

Although not located on my beloved Westgate Road, there was another family home that I spent a great deal of time in. Alden and Georgia Berry lived in a splendid house located on Freeman Hill, with their four children, Peter the only son, Bonnie, Carol, and Debbie who was my age. It was once the home of the author Winston Churchill, a member of the Cornish Colony and it also neighbored the house and studios of the famous painter Maxfield Parrish. The Berry's old mansion-style house, was enormous and contained many unique rooms that are still vivid in my memories. There was a beautiful library, stacked high with shelves of books. We played board games, dressed paper dolls and listened to countless songs on the old record player while sitting in this cozy setting. Their dining room held a large, long rectangular dining table, where I enjoyed many warm, friendly meals with their family. These meals were prepared in my favorite room in the house. There was something very special about Georgia Berry's kitchen; the warmth, the smells, and the memories of the many projects completed there; like making candles and other crafts under the gentle guidance of Debbie's mom. All adding to the charm, of this lovely old kitchen.

They had a large in-ground swimming pool, as mentioned before one of the very few in town. It sat a short walk from the house, surrounded by a thick, large, tall formal hedgerow, making it feel as though you were stepping into a magical kingdom as you entered the pool area through the opening in the vast shrubbery. There were a lot of stone paths and walls in the yard adding to its beauty. We enjoyed many warm summer days and nights in that pool, except on the not so rare occasion when a snake living among the stones decided to join us. I was plenty cool, after one of those unwelcome visitors arrived.

The Berrys operated a sheep farm on their property for about a decade. They had a herd of two hundred and fifty head. It was a family project, with all hands on deck. I was witness, to many a bleating sheep having its winter coat sheared to provide wool that was sold to a company in the Hillsborough area. How could that "yucky" wool coat, become such beautiful cloth?

During the times after the sad and early death of Mrs. Berry in 1968, I spent a lot of time with Deb and would learn through her sorrow and loneliness that life was not always fair. Her siblings were older, and away at school or off doing their own thing. She would often call me to come visit with her, especially on stormy nights. The wind would blow their stored items in the attic making eerie sounds, like those in a haunted house, the old windows and shutters would rattle and clang, and the lights would flicker easily. Not much fun, for a lonely, young teenage girl.

◇◇◇◇

The Chellis family became a special part of my life through my brief marriage to Michael, the eldest son of Frank and Vera. The twin boys, Tommy and David, shared with their older brother, their father's great sense of humor. Vera was a small built woman, whose loving ways were her only salvation in a house full of wayward male behaviors. Frank and his boys, were constantly playing practical jokes and making smart remarks. On one such occasion, one of the twins showed up to the dinner table without a shirt on. Frank admonished him about his improper table decorum and further asked him, "What would you think if your mother came to the table without a shirt on?" The twin replied by saying, "That it wouldn't matter much, it would be just like she was one of the boys." He was of course, referring to her very small figure.

David married, my friend and classmate, Cheyenne Sullivan, in 1974. I was their Matron of Honor and I have a picture with a really large hat on to prove it. Cheyenne and I continue to be dear friends, with too little time to share. We will forever share the sad bond of having each lost our only sibling at a much too young of age, to cancer. By caring for them in our homes during their last days, we both know in our hearts that we did all that we could to make their lives and deaths more bearable for them, and our families. It was also with a heavy heart, that I recently watched her bravely face the loss of her beloved David to cancer, again much too early. Now, sadly, she also faces this devastating disease as it plagues her own body for the second time. Even though, we are no longer bonded through marriage, we feel a sisterly tie that cannot be broken.

The Chellis family owned and operated a telephone company, that before converting to dial in 1973, still used a magneto switchboard, which sat in a small room off of the dining room in the family farmhouse. Their dining room has hosted countless and frequent family gatherings around their large, formal dining room table over the many years. So, whether it was a Sunday dinner, a holiday, or another special event, each gathering was met with the challenge of who was going to man the switchboard. Through the years, my husband of now nearly forty years, Sonny and I, have also shared meals around that family table.

Shortly before David died, he and I had a conversation about the old phone systems in town. We joked about how the kids, on my side of the town, thought our common battery phones were so much more modernized than their old, hand crank system. Their hand crank phones, on the eastern side of Plainfield, in the Village of Meriden, were connected through the operator manning the switchboard at the Chellis home. Our common battery phones were connected through the operators in Windsor, Vermont. These phones were an ugly black color, quite heavy, and had receivers that were cradled on the phone base, which was plugged into the wall with a very short cord. I'm not sure if the term portable phone, was even invented back then, you talked on the phone where it was connected to the wall. You also talked on the phone for about five minutes, because your neighbor might need the shared party line. They would of course, quickly let you know, by picking up their home phone and listening in on your conversation, while alerting you to their need to use the line. By the way, when the phone rang, you didn't rush to pick it up, because you had to wait and see if it was your ring, or someone else's. Originally, we had an eight party line, then there were four homes on our line. Our number was 321-W5. Our ring was two short, one long.

The Chellis family will always hold a dear spot in my heart.

◇◇◇◇

The well known McNamara Farm, "Macs Happy Acres," situated on the River Road bordering the Connecticut River, was the home and workplace for another exceptional family. Bill and Hazel McNamara and their children Anne, Barbara, Joyce, Thomas and Patrick, showed me and others the importance of working together and overcoming life's setbacks. Bill McNamara became disabled through a farm accident, but it did not stop him or his family, in the pursuit of their dreams of success. They were then, and continue to be now, a hard working family unit. They have expanded their land over the years to host a number of businesses and careers, which will provide a legacy for their young, and be an example to others.

Joyce was a friend and classmate, that I enjoyed spending time with, especially on the farm with her family. Joyce came back into my life in the 1980's, when she worked at the Sullivan County Extension Service serving as the 4-H Extension Agent. When my daughter, Tracey was growing up, she and I together, joined the Smiley 4-H Club in Claremont, New Hampshire, under the leadership of Sandy Mercier. Joyce was in attendance at many of our 4-H events during those years, where we had a chance to reconnect.

◇◇◇◇

The Raymond home was always open to the friends of their children. Bob and Betsy Raymond wore a smile as they welcomed the many and varying ages of kids walking through their door, who were coming to spend time with their children, Andy, Francetta, Lee and Michael. Several older teenage boys used to hang out in their driveway with Andy. Jonathan, who was once a boyfriend of mine, the Hendrick brothers, and others could most often be seen working on their motorcycles, while the girls walked by and giggled. The Raymond's also considered their two dogs to be part of the family. They are best described as "Mutt and Jeff," due to the fact that they were completely the opposite. Their lovable giant of a Saint Bernard, Sheba, always lumbered towards us in the excitement of seeing us arrive, whereas their also cherished, small Boston Terrier dog, Sniffles, always managed to pass gas and clear the room. Perhaps he was not as happy to see us.

Lee Raymond and I were friends throughout our childhood years, and were practically inseparable during our high school years. She wrote on her class picture that "we were like sisters." We shared many wonderful times together and with our other friends. The Raymond home was the scene for many sleepovers, which included times of eating ourselves silly on junk food, while listening to the crooning voice of Bobby Goldsboro and other artists of the era. There were many of those enjoyable moments in their living room, filled with giggling teenage girls. Long summer days at the swimming holes, winter sliding and skating parties, tea parties, and birthdays all were filled with Lee's laughter. She has the greatest laugh, which will ring in my mind always.

Her parents planned super birthday parties, which sometimes included winter swimming parties at an indoor pool. This was a little out of the ordinary, or should I say special, for those times. Unlike today, our birthday parties mostly meant, please come to my home, there will be a few balloons, that by the way, we blew up ourselves, we'll play lawn games or "pin the tail on the donkey," and eat some homemade cake and ice cream. Not today. Now, there are themed parties that carry the price tag of a theme park admission for the entire family, with all of the add on costs. The cake rivals a wedding cake, party favors are a must, and in general, the whole event follows the idea of "keeping up with the Jones," and never repeat a party theme that has been already given. We would have been in big trouble with that one. I should have seen this coming with my kids; the paper goods all had to match and be of the current popular cartoon character, and the character decorated cakes began to replace mom's lovingly homemade cake. This was also the time when McDonald's started offering birthday party packages, which I'll admit I took full advantage of for our children's parties.

While looking at pictures of my past birthday parties, with fond memories of the simple, but happy times, my mind wandered back to a birthday gift, that I once received from my parents. Do you remember this jingle? "Meet the Swinger, the Polaroid Swinger. Only nineteen dollars and ninety-five! Swing it up, yea, yea. It says "yes", yea, yea." My father loved cameras, so I was destined to own this beauty. It came in a black carry case, the size of a medium sized pocketbook. The film developed outside of the camera and then had to be coated with a sticky finisher, which was spread over the photo.

To this day, I can still feel my fingers stick together from that goo. There were other Polaroid cameras to come, that involved sticking the photos onto a cardboard backing so that they would not curl up. I have a lot of those crooked pictures with extra glue sticking out from the edges. I remember thinking, "Please give me back my Kodak Instamatic." I have been working on family albums, and in my opinion, the photography industry took a step backwards during that period of time during my youth. My ancestor's photos are of fairly good quality and have held up well. With today's technology photos can be made great, even if taken by a poor photographer, like myself. We don't often think about technology going backwards and how it can effect a whole generation, but the photos of my youth are certainly an example of how this can happen. They have not held up well to the test of time and sadly their quality is mediocre at best.

Lee and I recently revisited in conversation, the 1961 Plainfield Bicentennial Parade, when we dressed up like the "old days" in period dresses, to ride the float depicting the one room school house of years past. She told me that she had turned that dress into a Little Bo-Beep costume for her daughter. I was relieved to hear, that I am not the only keeper of those oldies, but goodies.

A Friend For Life
Sharing Our Early School Days

My very first, dearly held, lifelong friend belongs to the famous J. D. Salinger family, which in those days, his fame did not matter much to us kids, he was just Peggy's dad. Margaret, "Peggy," who I lovingly call, "Piggy," captured a special place in my heart from the moment we met at about age four. She lived in Cornish, where my mother cleaned house for her mother, Claire, a quiet and unassuming woman. Again, one of the benefits of this type of work was that Viola got to tag along with Mom. In the early years, Peggy and I played house, created great works of art on her large, double-sided art easel, and enjoyed other such childhood fun in the her playroom just off the tiny kitchen. Another favorite spot of ours, was the small loft above their living room. She had a beautiful, handmade, miniature dollhouse, and our young, but quite vibrant and active imaginations filled the rooms of that special treasure with hours of doll family fun.

Outside, we swung as high as our pumping feet would get us on the wooden swing, which hung by long rope handles attached to the large tree in their yard. The yard and their cute cottage style home, with its modest interior, sat well protected behind a very high, broad-board wooden fence. The height, length, and close proximity of each board to the next ensured the privacy that her dad desired. Their home was on a very narrow, dirt, country, back road, which had very little traffic, except from the neighbors, but he still felt the need for the wall of protection.

In the winter, we built snowmen and slid down the hill behind their house; it felt like it took forever to climb back up that hill that was carved out of the land so steeply that you had to practically crawl up it on hands and knees to keep from falling off, before finally reaching the top. Just so that we could just do it all over again, even though we knew that the ride back down, filled with the thrill of the sharp descent would only take seconds. Afterwards, we warmed up in the kitchen with delicious hot chocolate which we shared with her little brother Matthew, when he was old enough to join the "big kids."

As we grew older, we ventured further into the woods, closer to the forbidden cabin hidden within the forest walls, where her dad spent his days and nights writing. When we were feeling adventurous enough, we snuck around his cabin climbing on and around the wood stacked for his stove, making "quiet" sounds in our attempt to not be heard. He would come out to chase us away, but I never remember him being really mad at us. Occasionally, we would be invited in for a quick chat.

There was a gentle little stream that ran through their woods, and even better, on the path leading to the forbidden cabin, there was a foot bridge that crossed the stream. The stern warnings to stay out of the water followed me to the Salinger home, but as usual the lure of the flowing water was too much to resist. We would sit dangling our feet over the bridge by the hour, watching the water flow downstream, eating our bag lunches packed by Peggy's mom, and drinking coke from bottles chilled in the cool water of the stream, where her dad kept them. One beautiful spring day, when the stream ran with a swift current, I managed to lose a flip flop into the abyss below. How do you explain only one shoe? It certainly had nothing to do with the forbidden stream or the wet clothes we were wearing!

Peggy and I started our school years together at Mrs. Perry's Tiny Tot Nursery School, which consisted of both a nursery school and a kindergarten program. Mrs. Clara Perry operated this school out of her home in Cornish, just down the hill from my bestest friend, Piggy's home and just up from my grandparents' farm on Dodge Road. There was no formally funded public kindergarten. No offense to any of today's programs, but I'll bet you that Mrs. Perry's program would be hard to beat, even now. She was a peach, but no pushover. We learned to play "nicely," developed classroom manners, memorized nursery rhymes, recited our ABC'S, and learned about numbers. Friends during these years, included kids from both Plainfield and Cornish, from wealthier and not so wealthy families. A local boy, Butch Laurie, bears mentioning here, all of us girls loved him with his cute smile and long eye lashes.

Mrs. Perry transported students in her big station wagon, no matter the weather. We are talking about narrow, dirt, back roads with lots of hills, which in places climbed as steeply as rugged mountainsides. The roads would also gradually, but continuously climb up the long hillsides for miles. In the spring, they were muddy and riddled with washboard ridges that could shake any car off the road. In the winter, after the heavy New England snowstorms, the snow banks were piled high by the plows, about as tall as a one-story house. These roads which in normal conditions were barely wide enough for two cars to pass by each other, were often only passable in winter conditions, if one car pulled way over and stopped to let another pass. One snowy, winter morning, Mrs. Perry's station wagon went off the road into a deep, high, snow bank when she was trying to enter the steep, sharply curved entrance to the Farley estate. A local farmer with a team of oxen had to come pull us out, no emergency vehicles, no panic, just good ole country patience, and neighborly help. We kids were pretty excited about the whole event, I wonder if Mrs. Perry felt the same way.

Each year, a graduation celebration was held in the Blow-Me-Down Grange Hall on the stage with the back drop mural created by the artist, Lucia Fairchild Fuller, entitled "The Puritan Settlers." The nursery school students were promoted to kindergarten, and the kindergarteners donned in cap and gown, received their diplomas to move on to public school. I still treasure my Bachelor of Rhymes diploma with its colorful display of nursery rhymes and illustrations, just as much as my high school diploma and my college bachelor's degree.

After the tender years at Mrs. Perry's, came our first big day at the Plainfield Plain Elementary School, sitting proudly in the Village of Plainfield. To the eyes of the young, this large white building with its tall, long-paned glass windows looked a little overwhelming. A short stairway leading up from both sides to the middle front entrance opened up to a long hallway, which gave access to the four-room schoolhouse. Each classroom housing two grades. On the back side of the school, were the same high, large-paned windows which offered a view from the classrooms of the welcoming playground, that was just waiting to be filled with the laughter of children. Now looking at the building with adult eyes, I realize that its size is not quite as impressive, as it was to a six year old.

Down the hill we trekked into the loving arms of our first grade teacher, Mrs. Corette. Peggy described her special dress perfectly in her book <u>Dream Catcher: A Memoir</u>: "a pink-striped seersucker dress with two huge green frogs appliquéd on the skirt pockets." I can see Mrs. Corette standing there smiling brightly, just like it was yesterday. With her special touches she instilled the love of learning in all of her students, each and every day, while she filled our hearts with wonderful moments showing each of us how very important we were. On the occasion of each student's birthday, she held her precious, beautifully decorated, cardboard birthday cake while the whole class sang, "Happy Birthday" to the day's honoree. I believe that her smile made the paper candles light up each time. For Valentine's Day, we made frilly heart holders to hang on the back wall, where we proudly placed a personal valentine in every classmate's heart. She made sure that "no child was left behind," in every sense of its meaning, even those students without the means to buy cards, had them to share on this holiday. In later years, while working in a small classroom of wonderful children, I borrowed some of her loving ideas, like the valentine holders.

Our luck continued into the next year, as she also taught second grade in the same warm and welcoming classroom. Her students learned from the reading lessons taught using <u>Fun With Dick and Jane</u>, practicing memorization and repetition drills, while she displayed hours of patience. She served the children of Plainfield for 20 years (1953-1973). My sister, Carol, was blessed to have had her ten years after me. Mrs. Corette never forgot her students and kept up with their progress, well into her retirement years. It was not unusual, to receive a personal note from her about an event in your life.

We were promoted to the third grade, and into the kind and caring hands of Mrs. Beaupré. She too, lovingly nurtured her students and shared freely her generous smile. Through her lessons, she opened our eyes and minds to the world and all of the adventures awaiting us. She shared with us, her excitement of learning through reading, and discussing topics that interested the eager and growing minds of third-graders. She took us to exciting places, and helped us to meet people that we had not yet seen or met, through her enlightened instruction.

I can't recall exactly when, but we also had reading lessons in the basement classroom, with Mrs. Northrup. She taught different reading level groups throughout the day. Peggy and I were both avid readers, but we were also avid talkers. Mrs. Northrup had a chalk drawn box in the upper left hand corner of her blackboard, labeled "Noisy Box." Heading the list of names was always, Viola and Peggy. Did they have permanent markers then?

Another area of instruction that we received during these years bears a quick mention. Our Penmanship teacher, Mr. Robertson, came periodically to our school, like a traveling salesman, which was a little out of the ordinary. He was a very tall man, so tall, he had to bend down a little to write on the board. His long arms would make the words written in perfect form flow across the blackboard. The school should have saved their money with Peggy and me, we had poor penmanship then, and not much has improved over the years. He was a nice man, but we had better things to do with our time, and we were not accustomed to getting poor grades in any subject. "Remember Practice Makes Perfect!" This poor handwriting trait, I believe is hereditary; while at 4-H camp I would receive letters from my grandmother Atwood, but I had to wait for my mother to read them to me when my parents came to pick me up. How I laughed, years later, when we went to get our daughter, Tracey after a week at the same camp and she asked me to read Grammy Sawyer's (my mother) letters to her. Now, I try to write legibly to my sweet grandchildren.

Fourth grade led us to the room mastered by Miss Chapman. Have you ever played the card game, Old Maid? Peggy once again hit the nail on the head, with her description of Miss Chapman in her book Dream Catcher: A Memoir: "The old battle-ax, who looked like a gargoyle perched on the gates to every child's nightmares..." I will not even try to compete, but Miss Chapman was scary as hell, especially when she was mad. On one such occasion, she was quite upset with my behavior during one of her lessons, I believe that I was giggling, not an unusual occurrence, at someone's mischievous behavior. She shook me so hard that I wet my pants. I continued to giggle uncontrollably. As embarrassing as it must have been, I can only remember the outrageous giggle fit that I had. I still have those giggly fits periodically, thank goodness no pants wetting. Yet!

Our "senior year" at the Plainfield Plain School was the fifth grade, with teacher and school principal, Mrs. Spalding. As you might surmise, Peggy and I had already been introduced to the principal before. She was normally a stern and all-business teacher, but periodically she warmed up and let that great smile of hers slip out. I learned a great deal from her lessons. Peggy and I especially loved the SRA Reading Laboratory Kit, where each student continued on to higher reading levels at one's own individual pace, while further challenging us at each level. These self-paced levels were all color coded, which offered a visual path to our progress. This was all pretty neat to fifth-graders with a desire to excel. We let no grass grow under our feet with this task and Mrs. Spalding was likely happy that we were well occupied.

Not only were Peggy and I skilled readers, but we were also quite prolific with spit balls. Mrs. Spaulding, however, did not think that particular talent was beneficial to the learning environment. Our desks were located in the back of the classroom where most of the boys also sat. One day, while practicing our spit ball skills on the neighboring boys, Mrs. Spaulding's eagle eye caught us. Our normally good memories, could not remember having been warned about this behavior before, or so we wanted her to believe. Wasn't this our first offense? She kept us in for lunch recess. No! Not our favorite time of the day. Please! She distributed, by hand, hundreds of tiny, shredded pieces of paper all over the floor of her classroom. She had the pieces all primed and ready in her desk drawer. She must have been planning this little lesson for a long time. We were duly instructed to pick them up, one piece at a time. Did I say this was our first offense? One might think, that after this life lesson that we would have been cured of the desire to improve on our spit ball techniques. What do you think?

Recess indeed, was our most favorite time of the school day. I can't recall exactly how many recess periods that we had each day, but I think more than one, however the lunch recess was one glorious hour long. In some ways, it seemed that recess was endless as we played dreamily along with no sense of time, but of course, when the bell rang, it never seemed long enough. Now that I substitute teach, I realize that the playground teachers must have thought it was an eternity, especially during those cold, wintry New England days. I am thankful now, for only thirty minutes of recess duty. Most days, we ran for the swing set where we competed to be the highest swinger, and to see how far back we could lean, without breaking our necks. Over and over again, we would slide down the tall metal slide that burned our fannies and the backs of our legs on hot summer days, and sent us down it with the speed of lightning when it was slicked with wet snow, that turned to ice. We would spin ourselves silly on the merry-go-round, that sat low to the ground with metal bars criss-crossing it. We held onto those bars for dear life, while one or more of the older kids used the bars to propel the ride forward, while running in the well trodden path circling it. This experience offered thrills and life threatening falls. We found great fun, as well, on the long, wooden teeter-totter. We would hit the ground as hard as we could with our end of the board, trying to "buck off" the opposite rider. We would also make the board bounce by pushing off hard with our feet and try to make it skip to the next ridged section that was used for balancing the weight. When the playground equipment was not on our agenda, and we were deciding on what our the mood of the day was, we had plenty of activities to choose from. Besides the thrill of chasing after the boys to make sure that they paid attention to us, we also enjoyed playing 45's on our portable record players and dancing like we were on <u>American Bandstand</u>. Sometimes, a baseball game might be going on, or perhaps the chain for the almighty, "Red Rover, Red Rover, send Peggy right over" might be forming in the middle of the field. We enjoyed playing the ever popular games of cat's cradle, hopscotch, jacks, and jumping rope-- especially doubles. Do you remember those rhyming songs? "One pitcher, two, pitcher, three pitcher, four...," "Blue Bird, Blue Bird through my window...," "Mabel, Mabel, set the table...and don't forget the red hot peppers," "Bluebells, Cockle shells, Eevie, Ivy, Over...," "I love coffee, I love tea..."

Spring brought out the marble bags, or in some cases an old sock worked just as well to hold those treasured possessions. I still have a bag of marbles, and of course, among them are my most prized biggies, purees, and cat's eyes. Let's play Poison, remember it's for keepsies, and no fudging. The fuller your bag was, the more bragging rights you had. After a rainstorm, the marble pot was always full of muddy water, making it all the more exciting. I think I ruined a lot of shoe heels digging those holes. I never see kids playing marbles anymore. In fact now, playground activities are mostly organized by staff.

The all-time favorite recess activity for Peggy and me, was to play in the woods at the far end of the playground, where large pine trees grew creating a dark, secretive kingdom. About forty feet into the wooded area, at the back side of the woods, lay the forbidden bank, which was a very steep, cliff-like bank. This bank dropped sharply down to a small stream running nearby. On the furthest right-hand corner of the bank, there was a lot of sand, which made sliding down it a snap. The students were allowed to play in the woods within sight of the teachers, but what fun was that? We were never, never, to go over the bank. Chasing after a ball was no excuse. You can probably see us in your mind, as Peggy and I, disappeared over the bank to explore the stream below, and to look for the elusive quicksand that my mother continually warned us about. These were among the occasions, that we met Mrs. Spalding, in her role as principal. When we were playing nicely in the woods area, we built impressive homes, by sweeping the pine needles into borders using the pine boughs as brooms. We created room after room, each connected by pine needle-lined halls and doorways, for us to play house in. We never lacked for imagination, perhaps we should have become architects or home designers.

Peggy and I also managed to have Mrs. Spalding visit with us, from time to time, in the girl's bathroom, located in the basement. Her classroom was near the head of the stairs that led to the girl's bathroom, so she was within earshot of any heightened noise level in that area. I'm not sure how we managed so much bathroom time together. It was a great location for catching up on the latest news, or planning our next misadventure, but most importantly, were the times when we met to wash my hair on the day after my mother had given me one of her infamous Toni home perms. Why didn't she just stick my finger in a light socket and have it done with! Peggy and I would wash those curls over and over again, in the little porcelain sink trying to relax the frizz and get rid of the smell. The end result was just more curls, wet clothes, and oh yes, another chance to get to know Mrs. Spalding.

The basement of the school would not be likely described as bright and cheery, but rather drab and dreary. The basement was unfinished at best, with rough edges of granite boulders painted over with gray paint. The small, dimly lit bathrooms, roughly built storage and maintenance areas, were located in the center of the basement. Two large rooms sat at each end of the building, housing Mrs. Northrup's reading classroom on one end, and the lunchroom on the other. The lunchroom was also used for air raid drills, music, and band lessons. The thought of our school lunch program, elicits two thoughts, Yuck and more Yuck! I hated hot lunches. Were those really scalloped potatoes or just an excuse to get rid of the extra onions? It took me a long time, to develop any taste for some onion flavoring in my food.

I think back with great fondness about my school years in the 1960's, when our whole school would join in the celebrating and honoring of our country's history and what it stood for. We were proud to be Americans and proud of our wonderful and not-so-small-time town, Plainfield. Every day, our classes began with respectfully Pledging our Allegiance to the Flag, a sung prayer reminding us to be kind and good to others, and a selection of patriotic songs, such as: "The Star-Spangled Banner," "America the Beautiful," "My Country, 'Tis of Thee," "God Bless America," "This Land is Your Land," or "Yankee Doodle." They were proudly sung, with each student knowing the words by heart. Every year, we placed flags on the graves of the veterans for Memorial Day. Recitals were held in the front parking lot of the school, celebrating the holiday with music honoring our country and those who had served it. We practiced our performance for weeks, getting ready for the upcoming celebration. The distinctive high-pitched sounds of our tonettes making their presence known. How did our parents survive those hours of practice?

Memorial Day soon led to the end of the school year, and the ever anticipated summer vacation. Summertime, meant not only having all day to play at all of our favorite pastimes, but also, we looked ahead with great anticipation to the special event held each August. The biggest fair on Earth in our eyes, The Cornish Fair. This event offered excitement for all of the ages, each waiting to meet up with friends and reconnect with those not recently seen. There were agricultural events; that included animals to be judged, horse and oxen pulling, and displays of flowers and vegetables. Also on display, were the area's finest crafts created by the young and old, some with expert hands, and some by the those learning through organizations like my beloved 4-H. "I pledge my head to clearer thinking, my heart to greater loyalty, my hands to larger service, and my health to better living for my club, my community, and my country" and in later years they added "and to my World."

All of this was fun, but the real excitement for me lay in the midway; where the rides whirled round and round, filled with screaming kids. At night, the ride's lights illuminated the fairgrounds like a magical kingdom. My favorite ride was the swings. They made me feel so free, I especially loved to twist my dear, Peggy's swing round and round, and then watch her seat untwirl while we rode high above the crowds, with our feet dangling freely. There were also a host of carnival games, where you were quickly called to come join the fun, and then easily lost your money. If you were hungry, just follow your nose to the vendors selling french fries, hamburgers, hot dogs, sweet and syrupy Sno-cones-- that turned your mouth to the pretty color of your chosen flavor, candied apples, and oh my, that glorious sticky, sweet, pink, cotton candy that was twirled in delicate fluffy swirls around a paper tube. Should we ride the ferris wheel or the tilt n' puke, as we called it, so we can be sick after eating all of that greasy and sweet food?

Is it time for the parade? All aspects of country living were proudly displayed by the entrants. People representing organizations, would ride all dressed up in costumes on floats built by them, in accordance with that year's parade theme. Costumed kids would march or ride their bikes waving to the crowds lining the route.

Shriners paraded, some in their fast moving and quick turning carts, semis and motorcycles; while others in their elaborately costumed Oriental Band playing loud Middle Eastern musical instruments would entertain the on-lookers and scare the very young. Leaping Lena, an old jalopy filled with locals, would speed back and forth along the parade route. All the while, displaying the jalopy's ability to tip back and touch the road with its back fender, while the front end hovered above, looking like it might spill its passengers out at any moment. Local fire and police departments proudly presented their latest equipment, for all to see. Farmers drove their tractors, and animals were led by their owners eager to show them off. The parade watchers always looked forward to the teenaged girls riding on the back of the convertibles, dressed in their pretty gowns, waving as they passed by and hoping that they would be crowned as the next, Miss Cornish Fair.

Later, we would sit on the steep, dirt bank leading sharply up to the schoolhouse. The Cornish Elementary School is used as a part of the fairgrounds, for the display of the handmade items and locally grown products, waiting to be judged. Sitting under the tall white pines lining the steep bank, we would watch the scheduled shows including country bands, magicians, and other such talents brought in for the crowds enjoyment. We would anxiously await that evenings crowning of the new Miss Cornish Fair, a tradition dating back to 1958. As a young girl, I looked at the young women performing their talents and vying to be the next queen, with dreams that I might someday make the same stage. Then, at age seventeen, my dreams came true. I'm proud to wear the title of Miss Cornish Fair 1972. I also enjoyed a lovely reunion with the past queens in 1999, during the Fair's 50th Jubilee. Once again, riding in the parade and waving to the crowds.

Even though those glorious years of our youth have passed, Peggy and I still look forward to the Cornish Fair each year, sometimes we go, just to eat some of that great fair food. While other years, we have skipped the crowds and dust, to just float in the pool with a drink containing an umbrella, and reminisce about how much fun we had back in the day, roaming the fairgrounds.

Sadly, with our promotion to the sixth grade and the big move to the Meriden White School, my bestest buddy Peggy, was sent to another school. Please say it isn't so. Through the years, we have stayed in touch, coming in and out of each other's hectic and sometimes difficult life. No matter the time or the distance that has separated us, our bond has remained solid. She has been a vital source of strength for me, most especially through the worst time in my life, during the heartbreaking loss of my baby sister, Carol, to brain cancer.

Meriden White School

Fall arrived, and I was off to Meriden, to attend The White School. Unfortunately, I was going without my dear friend, Peggy. Luckily for me, I was destined to add to my circle of friends.

The Village of Meriden, within the town of Plainfield, bears explaining to the reader unfamiliar with its history. I will not even attempt to untangle the history involving the religious and political debates, that date back to the early times of Plainfield. What is important to my story, is that Plainfield and Meriden are one community, and my stories about friends and family involve both sides of the town.

Well, the Plainfield students heading to the sixth grade were big kids now, hopping on the bus in the Village of Plainfield, which on most days, required that we walk to the village to meet the bus. As was often said, to those of us who might complain about this hike, "When I was you're age, I walked three miles each way to school, no matter the weather." Often, the parents of many of us kids were already at work at this time of day, and the family did not have a second car, or in some cases, their parent still at home didn't drive a car. So, walking was a must. A quick note here, that will prompt the memories of many. The Goodyear Tire and Rubber Company in Windsor, was one of the places that my parents worked at, like many others did, from the area. They made rubber soles for shoes. Can your nostrils recall that smell? The glue alone, was enough to kill off brain cells. The odor permeated everything one wore or took into that plant. However, people did what they had to, in order to make a living, and the kids also did what was necessary, like walking to the bus stop. The kids heading off of the hill for the bus really did have a long walk, and it was in all types of weather. My thighs got frost bitten once, of course, I had a dress and fishnet stockings on.

Riding the bus was a new adventure for the Plainfield Village students. As usual, there were rules. The drivers, Bill Jordan, Forrest Chase, and "Big Bad John" Meyette were all well liked and respected townsmen. My father clearly explained to me, that he had better never get a call about my poor behavior on the bus, from one of his friends, the bus drivers. Wouldn't it be nice if all of the parents carried the same philosophy today. We sang on the bus and had fun, but when "Big Bad John" spoke, " We listened. Just like with " E. F. Hutton."

Our first year in the White School was the sixth grade, and we had a very pretty teacher by the name of Mrs. Burney. As should be expected, the work became more challenging and the subjects were broader, to start preparing us for the years ahead. It was a nice introduction to a new school.

Seventh Grade. Oh My! I'll leave the names out to protect the not-so innocent. Our teacher was a very tall, ruggedly built man who wore cowboy boots with long pointed tips. Let's say, that we had a few young men in our class, that had difficulty following the rules on a regular basis. They may have met their match here. There was a sizeable walk-in closet where the crank phone, still in use then, and supplies were kept. The naughty ones were sent to sit in this closet on a regular basis. I think they might call this a "time-out" spot these days. Additionally, being a very large man, he required a very large wooden desk with drawers. A student could easily fit under the desk and might come into contact with a certain pair of cowboy boots, if they were to move around too much, while sentenced to sit under the desk. Additionally, when the bottom drawer was opened slightly, it might possibly fit the head of a bent over student. Was this some sort of a punishment from the Colonial times, such as the stocks? In today's world, this would seem out of the question. Back then, if there were no real injuries, and there was a moment's peace in the classroom for learning; most parties believed that we would all survive the somewhat questionable methods.

I had a prized black and white striped shift dress that I liked to wear. He referred to me as, "Zebra." Even so, I still loved that dress. Funny how you recall such silly little things. My favorite subject that year was social studies, we had real projects that took weeks to complete (with no computers to do it for us). I still love projects!

Eighth grade was the very best. Mr. Steven Beaupré, the husband of our third grade teacher, taught 8th grade and he also served as the principal. Mr. Beaupré conducted the very best science experiments with us. He too, wore a great smile and shared it often. I'm not sure that the group of previously discussed young men got to see his nice smile that often. During this year, our English teacher left early and we were very fortunate to have had Mrs. Audrey Logan, step in and instruct us in English. She too, was a wonderful teacher, with a wealth of knowledge to share. The Tale of Two Cities and West Side Story were never better read and discussed by an 8th grade class, I'm sure of it. Denis Reisch joined the staff and enhanced the academics, as well as the physical education of the school. Like Mrs. Corette and the Beauprés, he too, would go on for years serving the students of Plainfield, including my sister Carol, some ten years later. I always told her, that I paved the way for her with these great teachers. I believe strongly, that the education we received from our not-so-small-time town of Plainfield, prepared us very well for our years at Lebanon High School, and beyond.

There were a lot of fun things to do during these school years. My love for books made the weekly class trips, by foot, to the

Meriden Library something to look forward to. There was one trip however, that was not so great. One of the young men in my class, yes one of those, decided to put a snake down the back of my shirt while walking back to school along the long school driveway, which was lined with a stone wall, where those slithery creatures lived. He got a little vacation from school for that nasty maneuver.

We worked on yearbook committees, the boys played organized sports against other schools, and the girls were cheerleaders-- pom-poms and all. "Rah Rah Ree, Kick him in the Knee, Rah Rah Rass, Kick him in the other knee." Best of all, each winter, a carnival of olympic proportions was held. We prepared for days, building snow sculptures, just like the big boys at Dartmouth College, which is located about ten miles north of Plainfield. I wonder if their water soaked mittens froze to their hands too. One year, my class built "Cousin Itt." I look at the pictures in our old school yearbook and realize how ugly that sculpture was, but we thought it was worthy of a first place prize. There were contests for skating and skiing, downhill as well as cross country, and ski-jumping. We went sliding and snowshoeing. It was a winter wonderland of activity, made even more special because Kimball Union Academy, then an all-boys private school, and an important part of Meriden's history, had state-of-the-art facilities that they shared, for our use.

As is usual for this adolescent stage, we all fell in and out of love, hundreds of times over the years. Going steady, holding hands, stealing kisses, fighting with your best friend over some boy (or girl), and the drama went on and on. My steady, was Rodney. Who is going steady with Mike O'Leary, David Grobe, Gary Williams, Francis Torrey, or Herbie Williams today? "It's my party and I'll cry if I want to…" "Now it's Judy's turn to cry…" "Will you please wear the gum wrapper, chain bracelet that I made for you?" Even with all of that pubescent trauma, the friendships blossomed.

Various groups hung out together at recess, playing, and planning their weekend fun. The girls had fabulous PJ parties, some at the Gibson home. Mrs. Gibson was mom to Lucy, Elaine and Marty, my once heart throb. She was then married to the minister of the Meriden Congregational Church. The church's parsonage had a large hall that we used to party in. Were we supposed to be having fun in there? Their mom loved to have us around. She truly enjoyed watching us teenaged, giggling, girls having the time of our lives. We made trips to buy treats at MacLeay's General Store, owned by Gardiner and Kay MacLeay, which was the social meeting place for residents living in the Village of Meriden.

Eighth grade graduation ceremonies were held in high esteem in those days. Ours was held in the front parking lot of the school, while the families looked on with great pride and "nightmares of college tuition dancing in their heads." There were award winning essays to be read, class wills to be handed down to the incoming class, and class gifts to be presented. These were gifts of meaning(sometimes jokes), versus value. I received two white plastic horses. It was the standing joke, that Viola would be in to school, as soon as she rounded up her loose horses. Why did they wait until I was already for school to put their escape plan into action? I wish that I had known about leg irons back then. I guess that it was just training for my future career in Corrections. Then came the final handshake, and beaming smile from Mr. Beaupré as he and Mr. Merrill, the Superintendent, shook our hands and handed us our diplomas. Was Mr. Beaupré smiling because he was proud of us, or happy that our class was moving on? Lebanon High School, here we come, the kids from a not-so-small-time town, Plainfield.

The Cornish-Windsor Covered Bridge spanning the Connecticut River
with Mt. Ascutney in the background
Photo taken by my father

View of Mt. Ascutney
Photo taken by my father

Read Family Farm in Plainfield
Photo taken by my father

Five generations at the Read Family Farm--1955
L-R May Read Atwood (grandmother) Lena Rogers Read (great-grandmother)
Louise Atwood Sawyer (mother) Viola being held by her
great-great grandmother Addie Rounds Rogers

Five generations--taken on Viola's 2nd Birthday--1957
L-R Louise Atwood Sawyer   May Read Atwood
Addie Rounds Roger
Viola sitting on the lap of Lena Rogers Read

Viola sitting on the stairs of the farmhouse that burned down at
"Grandpa Mick's" Farm--Hartford, Vermont

Viola with her father -- Grandparent's (Sawyer) New Moon Trailer
Woodstock, Vermont

The Crooked Little House -- Bill Greene's Rare Bird and Animal Farm
Viola with her little cousins--Sharon and Linda Spaulding

Grandpa Jack Sawyer playing Santa
for Viola in her Plainfield trailer

Don MacLeay with his Piper Cub

Bernard and Mildred Eaton
With a lucky canine border at their "Doggie Motel"
Photo courtesy of Debra Dion Krischke

Vacant Barn on Grandparent's (Atwood) Farm Property
Next to my house-- my daytime play area and the setting for my nightmares
Courtesy of Debra Dion Krischke

My daughter Tracey receiving a 4-H award
from Joyce McNamara Judy

Mrs. Clara Perry awarding Viola her diploma from Kindergarten from the Tiny Tot Nursery School
Unfortunately, the beautiful mural is covered by a curtain.

Peggy Salinger and Viola --Graduation from Kindergarten
You'll note in all of the photos of us that we are, were much taller than most other kid's our age.

Viola with her sister Carol and Mrs. Corette--1st Grade teacher to both of us
Taken at my sister's graduation from 8th Grade

Viola' birthday party-1st Grade - Left front L-R: Joyce McNamara, Sharon Spaulding-cousin, Debbie Dion - Back L-R: Wendy Reed, Linda Spaulding--cousin, Marilyn Perry - Standing right rear: Viola and Peggy, In front: Kelly Atwood--cousin

Viola and Peggy - Plainfield Plain School -Memorial Day Recital playing a duet on our tonettes

Viola and Peggy--Cornish Fair Midway
enjoying candy apples on the ferris wheel

Viola's birthday party-- in my New Home--nine years old
L-R -Jean LaPan, Debbie Berry, Viola, Wendy Reed, Mary-Jo Barto, Shirley Stone

They Are Not Just Buildings

Thus far, my story has spoken of the unique geological history that formed the beautiful and useful lands, that then led to the inhabiting of it by the settlers, in 1761. A landscape, so impressive, it has beckoned many people over the years. These people have come from varied backgrounds and ways of life. Yet, they all were drawn to this very special place. All of this history, set the foundation for future generations of families to also call our not-so-small-time town of Plainfield, their home. I have shared my family history and the personal stories that filled my childhood years. As well, I have told of the significant role that many other families and individuals have played in my life and the importance of their nurturing of me during my youth.

Our village life, also included some notable and distinctive buildings, that I spent countless hours in, over the years. Plainfield, has a wonderful historic presence in its impressively designed buildings, many with an architectural significance belonging to the era in which they were built. These highly regarded buildings have been, and continue today, to be the gathering spots for important town and family events, year after year, and generation after generation.

The Plainfield General Store

The Plainfield General Store was built in 1905, a striking three story structure, that served as the central social hub of our community. Just about everyone in town made a least one trip to the store a day, some by foot, others by car, kids on bicycles, and Viola on her horse. Just like the old west, there was a hitching post for the horseback riders.

Where do I begin? Where all children would, at the candy counter. That magnificent glass display case was filled with morsel after morsel of penny candy: bubble gum cigars of various colors, Bazooka Joe gum wrapped in comic paper, sweet Fruit-Striped gum, boxes of candy cigarettes, hot fire balls, Pixie Sticks filled with varying colors of pure sugar, tiny wax bottles filled with colored sugar water, Tootsie Pops with their deliciously filled centers, and bright red wax lips, as well as, white wax teeth just waiting to be chewed into a ball of sweet bliss. Maybe, the baseball cards attached to my bicycle spokes with clothespins need replacing, so I'll buy a package of gum, complete with those "useless" cards. How wealthy could I be today, if I had only saved those collectible cards instead! When you were feeling particularly rich; the nickel, full size candy bars, filled your eyes with plenty of choices.

The ice cream cooler also called out to me, especially on hot days. Perhaps, I'll have a Creamsicle, Popsicle, Fudgesicle, chocolate or strawberry sundae on a stick, a Rocket, an Eskimo pie, an ice cream sandwich, or possibly a Dixie Cup-- complete with a wooden spoon. So many choices, so little change.

Thirsty? No aluminum cans or plastic here. Your soft drinks came in heavy glass bottles with a metal cap that had to be opened with a "church key." " What will hit the spot today?", maybe a Pepsi-cola, Coca-Cola, or a Hires Root Beer, or perhaps a Cream soda, Orange or Grape Crush, if not, maybe Fruit Punch, a Moxie or even that dark colored Ginger ale-- which had a much stronger taste back then.

Now, that I am more familiar with marketing skills, I realize that it was in full force at the store. While waiting to pay for your goods, there were many temptations staring you in the eye. As you stood at the counter, you were faced with large jars filled with items luring you in, depending on your individual tastes. I'll start with my favorite one, the fat, chocolate covered cream drops that would melt in your mouth. Yum! For the palate desiring a stronger taste; there were pickled eggs, red pickled sausages, beef jerky and Slim Jims. My eyes were always drawn to the huge wheel of cheese, calling my name from under the large glass dome that was keeping it fresh. How I loved that cheese! "Can I please have a slab today?" When given the go ahead, I would eagerly wait, while it was wrapped in the white paper, torn from the massive roll used for wrapping meats and then neatly tied off with string winding from the large spool hanging overhead. There were no computers or calculators used to ring up your purchases, just a big old adding machine, or sometimes only paper and pencil. They knew how to make change, too. Even better, we kids knew what we had for money to spend, how to add up our purchases, and count our change back. "Would you like me to put this on your account?" Imagine trying to run a tab at a store today.

The store's shelves were stacked high with all of the general items one might need, because it was a long drive to Windsor or West Lebanon. Those trips were saved for shopping day excursions to visit the Super Duper or the A&P. I would look forward to receiving the trading stamps, earned from our purchases on those trips: S&H Green, Top Value, Gold Bond or Plaid. We couldn't wait to fill up those coupon books. "What are we saving for this time? Let's look in the <u>Big Idea Book</u>." Sometimes, trips to the store were not necessary, the goods were brought to you. If you were lucky to be on the route, the milkman delivered to your door, fresh milk in glass bottles covered by a cardboard stop. They were left by your door in a metal rack, and in later years, the more modern aluminum, insulated box. You had to remember to shake the bottle before using the milk, to mix in the cream that had settled to the top. A note was left, in an empty bottle being returned to the milkman, which told him what you wanted delivered the next time. "Will the Sunbeam bread man be here today?"

The townspeople visited the store for just about everything, including gassing up their cars. The store's old Texaco gas pumps whirled to fill the empty tanks. Nearly everyone was a regular at the store, but some were daily visitors. It was told, that dear Mrs. Jenney, wife to Bill, who owned the Jenney Potato Business, used to go the store three times daily to purchase what she needed for their next meal. If the story holds true, she certainly supported the local economy and her family had fresh meals. Who cares, as long as she brought along one of those cute Jenney boys!

One reason that the store was well visited, was the fact that it also served as the post office. If you forgot your key, no problem, your mail was happily given to you. Unlike today, when it's rare to receive no mail on any given day, there was no junk mail. Many days, I would peer into the window of old box #47 only to be disappointed by the empty slot, but I never gave up. Eventually, there would be mail for me, from my grandparents or my dear friend, Peggy. In later years, naturally there were the awaited letters from certain young men.

Steve and Doris Plummer were the owners, who had run the store since 1923. Steve's brother, Max worked for them as well. The Plummer family home sits in the village nestled between the church parsonage and the library. The Plummer name then, as well as today, is well known for being someone who is a vital member of the community. So it was big news, when in 1961, the Barto family from New York City, was moving to town to take over the operations of the store and there would be a new postmaster to handle our precious mail. It turned out for me, that this was not only big news, but a great beginning in yet another chapter in my life. The Barto family could have easily been included in my chapter on the Plainfield families that had a strong influence on my life, but the Bartos are the Plainfield Store to me, so they belong with this part of my story.

Jim and Flo Barto, and their two youngest daughters, Linda and my new friend Mary-Jo, moved into the home above the store. Their eldest daughter, Jerri, remained in New York with her family. She was a professional dancer. Mary-Jo's and my quickly formed friendship led us to be college roommates and continues long distance today. Visiting the Barto home was always an exciting adventure and often included other kids. Lee Raymond, Danny MacLeay, Shirley Stone, and Julie Perkins were among the circle of friends who spent time there on a regular basis. The best place for group playing was in the attic, which was equipped with every doll and play kitchen accessory ever needed to entertain an eager bunch of kids. I believe we hosted tea parties grand enough for the Queen Mum herself. Mary-Jo's collection of fine toys to play with were not limited to the attic. She had the very best collection of stuffed animals these eyes had ever seen, among which, was a large cuddly alligator. I bought my grandson, Brady, one just like it years later. I still cuddle with his when I can. Neatly arranged and labeled in a special carrying case was as a selection of 45's, which offered hours of listening pleasure. I must admit, I was quite envious of her many treasures and thankful that she so willingly shared them with me and others. This quality, I am sure, was a result of her parents generosity and kindness towards others. Mrs. Barto was the dearly loved "Mrs. Cleaver" of those days. They may have come from New York City, but they sure did fit right into our not-so-small-time town, of Plainfield.

    Mary-Jo and I, along with others, spent endless hours at the swimming holes, tubing the Blow-Me-Down, ice skating, and exploring the woods, in all seasons. She and I especially liked to traipse the area off of the old dirt road that ran alongside the store and down over a small knoll into a wonderland of swamps and woods. We enjoyed traveling an old abandoned road hidden under the overgrown brush. This concealed route ran up over the hill and connected with the Freeman Road. There were some adult restrictions to be adhered to: the usual instruction of stay out of the water and an additional one of DO NOT go near that "old man's" cabin in the woods. What a perfect invitation to go see what was so forbidden. That dear "old man" just loved our company. I'm not sure how long he had lived his solitary life in this cabin, but it served as his home for many years. He reminded me of my "Grandpa Mick." His place even had the same smoky-wood smells. In the wintertime, we spent our hours in these woods blazing trails through the snow with our cross country skis or snowshoes. We put on a lot of miles in this area, in all seasons, and somehow never got lost. We must have had a built in GPS!

    We also shared a love of motorcycles and by the time we reached sixteen, we each owned a bike. Mine was a Bridgestone 90, and hers was a pretty gold colored Yamaha. We rode with our hair flowing in the wind, feeling free as a bird. Yet, another taste of freedom. The only thing missing were the flying colors, of our gang of two. I continued to ride a motorcycle for many years, now I feel lucky when I keep my bicycle upright.

There was another small store, operated by our school principal, Emma Spalding's husband, Tracy. This store, was known at one time, as Streeter's Store. I'm not sure what year it closed, but I remember how sad that building looked, with it's big empty windows. I'm glad to see it occupied now and once again a vital part of the community. In addition to basic supplies, this store carried items such as hardware and sporting supplies. The Spaldings' large, Federal style, brick home, known as the Silas Read House, sat on the lot between the two stores. On Halloween night, the line to their door was long. We stood there in our homemade costumes, holding our pillow cases already laden with sweet goodies from every house, on every road, that we could reach on foot. We waited anxiously, to be the next one in line as the Spaldings welcomed us into their kitchen. You were well received, even if you had been naughty in school that day. On their kitchen counter, would be box after box, of those coveted full size, nickel candy bars: Hershey bars, Milkyways, Snickers, Sky Bars, Butterfingers, Bit-O- Honey, large Tootsie Rolls, Almond Joys, and Mounds. "Sometimes you feel like a nut, sometimes you don't."

The Plainfield Community Baptist Church

The Plainfield Community Baptist Church is a brick structure, built in 1840, that sits in the heart of the Plainfield Village, next to the general store run by the Bartos. The lovely stained glass front window offers a welcoming sign for all to enter through one of the two wide front doors. The entrance hall leads into the sanctuary, where on sunny days the bright sun shines in through the tall glass-paned windows and warms the rows of mahogany pews. The Church has been renovated throughout the years to include the steeple section and the addition of a community area, named Pierce Hall, located in the basement. I loved hearing the clear sound of the sweet bells tolling and calling us to worship.

The church was an integral part of my life. I was baptized in this Church, when I was ten years old. My baby sister, Carol, who was born in 1964, and I were baptized together. I think that I may have been "put out" at the time, that I had not been baptized as a baby. I am, however, thankful that it did not take place in the 1920's, when baptism by immersion took place in the Blow-Me-Down Brook. Now, I have added this memory to my many cherished moments shared with Carol.

Reverend Hazel Roper, became the pastor of our church, in 1964. She had a strong commitment to the church and the community as a whole, with a special place in her heart for the youth. Her unique voice with its deep tones, resonates in my mind from time to time and I am brought back to that special period in my life where I felt a strong connection with those around me in a very special not-so-small-time town.

My parents did not attend church on a regular basis, so I can't recall exactly how I became so involved, but I attended Sunday school faithfully for many years. The lessons taught lovingly by so many members of the community were fun and life enduring. Pierce Hall was filled with music and the laughter of many children each Sunday. This small area was shared by many different age levels, but no one minded the cramped space. In our teen years, we graduated to the loft, which from the back of the church overlooks the sanctuary. Here, Mr. Overman patiently shared his knowledge and love of God with us. Thinking about the age and dynamics of our group, he must have been a saint.

The Overman Family was not just a very important part of my church life, I also spent a great deal of time in their home. They lived on Route 12-A, just over the Cornish town line. Their home was always bustling with chores: tending to the large vegetable garden, collecting eggs from the henhouse, and feeding the animals. Mr. Overman and their son Mark, were busy doing carpentry in their workshop, while Mrs. Overman and their daughter Jane, always had something cooking in the house. My favorite "chore" was making homemade root beer, the smell and taste of this refreshment still lingers in my mind, all these years later. Unlike the sweet taste of today's flavor, it had a strong taste, something on line of Moxie. One particular specialty of Mrs. Overman's cooking, was a baked apple that she sliced and somehow colored a pretty deep red. They were served as a side relish dish and tasted great, I think there may have been a hint of cinnamon in the taste. I wish I knew what they were called, I'd take a stab at preparing them. I shared many meals at their dinner table, you'll notice that trend throughout my home visits. I was an adept scout, seeking out all the great cooks in town and finding comfort food at their tables. As I said, my parents were not well off and my mother worked outside of the home. In fact, I do not ever recall her not working. My father often found himself between jobs and by default assumed much of the cooking, which he insisted, was to be eaten. I could perhaps write a book on how many ways you could prepare Spam or how many different recipes include the ingredient peanut butter. Another delicacy or two, which often found their way to the dinner table, were chipped beef and gravy (just for fun let's throw in a boiled egg or two) or a dish that was called Salmon Pea Wiggle, only their was no salmon. This meal was also a white gravy-based dish that was served over saltines, toast or mashed potato. Unfortunately, in our house, dark, oily, canned tuna was substituted for the salmon. Anyone, hungry?

In my teen years, Jane Overman and I, rode around in her snazzy, glacier blue Chevrolet Impala Coupe. We were always ready to hit the road. I was a member of her wedding party when she married. I also have a picture from this event showing off the "stylish" bridesmaid dress of the early seventies, complete with an empire top, heavily bordered by a wide band of velvet that wound around me just under the bust line and joined on the backside with a large bow accenting my rear-end. Neither of these areas, did I need to accent!

The Overman's also touched my family's life through Mr. Overman's building business. My dad worked for him in the late 1950's, and helped him build the garage that housed the Plainfield Sales and Service. I have home movie footage of the garage being built. My friend and nursery school classmate, Zoe Mace's dad, Nathan managed the garage. Mr. Mace's former garage sat down in the hollow just across the road and was taken down as a result of the newly revamped Route 12-A. Mr. Overman also built our home on Westgate Road, in 1962.

In addition to our Sunday School teacher's like Mr. Overman, and our Pastor, Ms. Roper, there were other members of the church who were committed to and involved with the youth. We had an active youth program which consisted of both junior and senior groups, depending upon your age. We participated in various activities to promote fellowship and a sense of community. They included year round outdoor activities, projects for individual and community purposes, bowling outings, and trips to events and special places. One such time, we journeyed to the Lebanon Opera House, that then housed the movie theater. Among the chaperones that I recall, were Ms. Roper, Mrs. Anita Morse, mother to cute, flirty Jonathan, and my mom. The movie of choice for us to go see was entitled, <u>A Thousand Clowns,</u> starring Jason Robards and Nick Gordon. In the 1960's, the movie review system was not as informative as it is today, therefore the adults must have truly thought that the movie was about clowns. I hope that the reader has seen this movie, so that you can really enjoy this. Briefly, this movie is about a twelve year old boy who goes to live with his eccentric Uncle Murray, in his bachelor apartment, in New York City. This child custody arrangement is being investigated by Child Services. During a visit to the apartment, the social worker inquires as to what kind of activities they engage in. The boy responds, that his favorite game is "Bubbles" and he produces a female statute with a large, bare bust, that lights up. "Yes Sir, "that's My Baby." I don't think that my mother and her chaperone companions could have shrunk any closer to the floor. Needless to say, we laughed hysterically at this part and at the red-faced adults. Did they ever take us to the movies again?

The youth also contributed on a regular basis to the Sunday service, assisting the Pastor. Preparing for our roles and sharing with the congregation was a meaningful experience, sometimes we contributed in a small way, such as with a reading, and on other occasions we led the entire service. I led the Sunday service just before leaving for college, in the fall of 1972.

Music was a wonderful addition to the Sunday service and other special services of the religious calendar. Mrs. Priscilla Hodgeman and later Mrs. Alice Hendrick, faithfully served the church with their musical talents on the piano and organ. Participation in the choir was also an avenue to connect and share with the congregation. I loved spending this time with my cousin, Linda Shepard, who had a lovely soprano voice. Mr. Overman was often the lone male voice, but always added his strong vocal chords to round off the harmony of those beautiful hymns. During the Christmas season, I enjoyed our caroling parties, where we traveled to homes sharing the joyful sounds of the holiday music. I especially loved to go to the nursing home, on Thrasher Road, in nearby Cornish. The residents' faces lit up like the lights on a Christmas tree, with our arrival to this stately old house, which was once the home of Bobby Barrows, another one of my Tiny Tot Nursery School classmates. Annual Christmas parties brought Santa, who would come to listen to all of the boys and girls recite their Christmas wish-lists, to find out if we had been naughty or nice, and to bring us gifts. Imagine my dismay, when on one December eve, I discovered that Santa was wearing my Dad's shoes! HO!HO!HO! There were a lot of tears. Santa Claus was a fake and my dad was in on it.

I looked forward each summer, to joining the church hosted Vacation Bible School, which was always well attended by many of the local children. Church life also included many other activities to help out on, such as: bake sales, church suppers, and wedding or funeral receptions. These were opportunities where men, women, and children all worked together to do God's work.

Early adulthood offered me yet another way to belong to the church, through the formation of the "Candlelighters." This group, under Ms. Roper's direction, was led in Bible study, performed community projects, and enjoyed mutual fellowship. All of which, helped us grow in our Christian life and added to the not-so-small-time town experience and lessons that I still carry with me today.

The Blow-Me-Down Grange Hall

"The Grange" is a shortened term, standing for the formal name of the National Grange of the Orders of Patrons of Husbandry. This grassroots, fraternal organization was formed in 1867, when American farmers saw the need to come together to promote and ensure their well being, concerning nationally recognized economic and political agendas. The Blow-Me-Down Grange Hall, also sits in the heart of the village of Plainfield. This Greek Revival style brick building, was built in 1839, and first served as The Old South Church. It was purchased by the Blow-Me-Down Grange No.234, a member of the Mascoma Ponoma Grange, in 1899.

The Grange was well-known for its political clout. I am told, that it was common knowledge in earlier times, that officers in the New Hampshire State Grange, were being groomed for political positions, including that of governor. It was definitely a prestigious organization of the times, and continues to be the oldest agricultural organization in existence today. Being farmers and politically motivated citizens, generations of family members, on my mother's side, were members of the Grange.

My great-great-grandparents, Fred and Addie (Rounds) Rogers, were very active in Grange business. They owned and operated a boarding house, known as the Cloverland Farm, in Meriden. They lured summer tourists to the boarding house, by touting beautiful views, fresh spring water, and bountiful fresh meals. Fred Rogers served the Grange on the local level, was Master of the New Hampshire State Grange, and held the position of Gatekeeper for the National Grange. He was also an elected representative to the New Hampshire General Court, and through his lobbying efforts in the early 1900's, was instrumental in the eventual establishment of the New Hampshire State Police.

My great-grandparents, Palmer C. Sr. and Lena (Rogers) Read, both held offices at the local and state level of the Grange, and also both served as representatives to the New Hampshire State Legislature. My great-grandmother was the first woman from Sullivan County, to be elected to the State Senate and to sit on a superior court jury. She successfully proposed legislation in 1943, to free the Cornish-Windsor Covered Bridge from toll charges. This magnificent bridge is now on the list of National Historic Places, and it is the longest, single span, covered bridge in the United States, that is open to car traffic.

My grandparents, Francis E. and May (Read) Atwood, also belonged to the Grange and served both the local and state Grange. Although, not an active participant, my mother, Louise (Atwood) Sawyer, continues to be a member of the Grange. I think that I belonged to every organization known to Plainfield during those years, but regretfully I never became a member of the Grange. I did however, attend many functions over the years with my family, both in Plainfield and other halls across New Hampshire and Vermont, connecting me to those villages of people.

The Grange Hall under went renovations throughout the years, which included the addition of the lovely mural painting, "The Puritan Settlers" by the artist Lucia Fairchild Fuller, a member of the Cornish Colony. This mural serves as a backdrop to the low stage, which is located on the second floor, overlooking the large meeting room, and where I celebrated my Kindergarten graduation.

The old kitchen of the Grange Hall, in those days, had none of today's modern conveniences. The kitchen and the dining room it serves, are located on the first floor and were always busy with activity when I was growing up. Generations of people, from near and afar, have attended functions in this hall, such as: grange suppers, community events, family reunions and wedding receptions. Also, located on the first level, in the back of the hall behind the kitchen, is where the then, in use and dreaded "two holer" was located. I won't even get into the pleasantries of this "pit stop," but I think as a young child I might have been traumatized at the thought of falling into that abyss. I can still wait a long time to use the potty, if I have to.

This long-standing hall was placed on the National Register of Historic Places, in 2001. Its organization has withstood the test of time, declining Grange membership, and thus a weak economic base. Its continuing existence is due to the love, hard work, and generosity of many people ensuring its existence. I am very thankful for this, as have I spent, and still do enjoy from time to time, many wonderful times there celebrating special occasions.

One of my more memorable events, was a Social Box Luncheon held for Valentine's Day. I was really quite young at this time, maybe about seven or eight, but somehow I wormed my way into being able to participate with the teenage girls in this social. I imagine they just loved that. The young ladies of the town prepared delicious box lunches for two and placed them in beautifully decorated boxes. Their names were hidden under the box, and the young men could place bids on them. The winners of each bid accordingly enjoyed their meal and time with the young lady who had prepared it. I was delighted to share my Social Box, teddy bear and all, with the "lucky" handsome bidder. He was likely longing to share his time with another young lady, but nonetheless, he was a gentleman about it. Besides, he got a great lunch.

The Plainfield Town Hall

The magic of the Plainfield Town Hall lies inside its doors and the history behind it becoming registered as a National Historic Place, and also on the List of National Historic Theaters. From the outside, the building appears rather plain and nondescript, except for its size. After passing through the small entryway, with a tiny kitchen area to the right, you enter a large hall, where facing you is an impressive stage with an amazing stage set. In 1916, during the Cornish Colony era, William Howard Hart, a painter himself, donated the funds to complete a professional stage set, with lighting, in the town hall. The famous painter, Maxfield Parrish, who resided and had his studio in Plainfield, was commissioned to create the stage set. The ever impressive, Mt. Ascutney is portrayed in the background of this magnificent piece of artwork, with the Connecticut River lying center stage encompassed with overhanging trees. Beautiful white birches and maple trees with their gloriously vibrant colors, growing mingled amongst granite rocks, are all adding to the beauty of the scene. The lighting provides for distinct settings to portray the various times of the day. The full light set displays a bright, clear scene, while at dusk the blue colors, that Parrish is famous for, dominate the stage set. Red and yellow hues from the lights, are emitted at varying degrees and offer brilliant scenes as well, while the all red lights, create an ethereal night view. This unique stage setting has been used for many plays over the years, by all ages of local groups, as well as, by members of the Cornish Colony. The stage set was restored in 1993, through the determination and hard work of community members. If you ever find yourself in our not-so-small-time town, this is a must see.

Behind the stage, there is a set of storage rooms for props and costumes. My great-uncle Abe, let my son Cory, borrow costume pieces for his role in a play while in the sixth grade. Even at his young age, he was impressed with the history that is stored there. The infamous "two holer," is also located in this area. No need to linger there. Over the front section of the hall is a small room accessed by a staircase. It was once used, for the town library and later the town selectman met there. Many of my relatives served as selectmen to the town, dating as far back as the early 1800's. My grandfather, Francis E. Atwood, served terms from 1944 to 1949.

The Plainfield Town Hall was originally built in 1798, at its first site on the Center-of-Town Road. The building was then moved twice, ending up at its current location in the Plainfield Village. Since it was rebuilt in 1846, it has hosted may events over the years, from town business being conducted to social events being held. Basketball games, school plays, and music recitals are among the memories of many. Square dances were a regular festivity, with the long wooden benches lining the outside walls, filled with eager dancers of all ages, waiting for room on the dance floor to swing their partners. Generations of Plainfield families have tapped their feet to the lively music and the square dance calls echoing from this hall. I think, if we listen carefully, we can still hear Don MacLeay's steel guitar, joined by his band partners of "Woody and the Ramblers" including, Sookie Morse on the organ, playing their hearts out to the "Virginia Reel."

The Mothers' and Daughters' Clubhouse

This unique and quaint Bungalow-style clubhouse, was designed by Charles A. Platt, a well known architect and member of the Cornish Colony. It was built in 1902, under the direction of a local resident, George Ruggles, who worked as a carpenter for Maxfield Parrish, and also supervised the building of Parrish's Plainfield estate, The Oaks.

The Mothers' and Daughters' Clubhouse, was the meeting home for, a group of both local women, and those from the Cornish Colony. These women felt that they could learn from each other, as well as, work together for the common good of others. One of their early ventures was a rug making industry which helped to finance their endeavors. Through the years, many social causes were supported through these efforts. The clubhouse now contains collections from Plainfield's history, carefully overseen by the members of the Plainfield Historical Society. The supporters of this building worked hard to secure its name on the National Register of Historic Places.

The homey atmosphere of this small bungalow, with its decorative wallpaper of the era, paintings that are encased in ornate frames, and heavy, long, flowered window dressings, has been the setting for many big milestones throughout time, for my family, as well as others. We have celebrated events such as weddings, anniversaries, and engagement parties at this small, but cozy site. I can still see my great-grandmother, grandmother, mother, and other female relatives, aproned and working in the small kitchen area near the backend of the room. Like the other kitchens in these old buildings, there was no running water. The old hand water pump stood ready to be primed and spew forth that fresh, clear, cold, spring-fed, well water, which of course had to be heated on the old stove to wash the dishes.

The bathroom facilities mirrored the other buildings as well, That's right the good ole "two holer." By the way, have you ever used one? In the winter? These "bathrooms" are not heated. This time, I will linger here to tell you a funny story. As I have indicated, my ancestors (The Reads) were heavily involved in local and state politics, and in early years were seen as quite influential in Plainfield. My father used to tell of the time, that he and Gordon (Tuffy) Spaulding, who was married to my mother's cousin Nancy (Wilder), were using the said facilities, where upon they began discussing a white flag propped in the corner. My dad said to Tuffy, "What do you suppose that white flag represents?" Tuffy responded, "Well of course, it was used when Plainfield surrendered to the Reads!" The family politics were often the butt of jokes, especially from the in-laws. I hate to use the word butt here, because it seems in poor taste. However, it does elicit another topic of family jokes, about having no difficulty recognizing the Read women, from behind. In 1990, while celebrating the Fourth of July, our family built a float, around the theme of "The Changing Times of the Read Generations." Don MacLeay, who at the time owned the Blow-Me-Down Farm, was kind enough to let us use his construction equipment to build our float on. The trailer had a large, conspicuous sign that cautioned--WIDE LOAD. So, several generations of us Read women, posed for a photo-op with this sign, and you can probably guess at what angle. The photo came out great, but it seems to have disappeared since then. Sorry, I would have included it.

The Philip Read Memorial Library

You guessed it, the library is named after a relative of mine. In 1920, Edmund S. Read, donated the resources to build the original library. He gifted the monies to Plainfield, in honor of his father, Philip Read. Philip was the son of my great-great-great-great-great grandfather, David Read, and his second wife. David was remarried, after the passing of his first wife, my great-great-great-great-great grandmother, Hannah (Kenney) Read. His second wife, who was also named Hannah (Jirauld), was the mother of Edmund.

The Colonial style, red brick library, with it's welcoming front portico, was a place of refuge for me. My love for books has been lifelong, and I believe that, in many ways, the warm atmosphere of the library with its beautiful mantled fireplace, likely added to this desire for reading. Browsing with the world at your fingertips is a wonderful feeling.

During the summer months, the library would offer the "Bookworm Reading Contest," for avid readers. I still have my ceramic bookworm that I earned, for reading the most books one year. How I loved to see that library loan card fill up.

In 2004, again through the efforts of community members, an impressive addition was made to the original library. There was a rededication ceremony held that year, and my grandmother May (Read) Atwood's, two surviving sisters, Kate (Read) Wilder Gauthier and Jean (Read) Hebert, were honored as relatives of Philip Read. There will be countless generations of readers who will dream big amongst those well stocked shelves of words.

As I complete this chapter, about all of the priceless buildings, that I and many others were so very fortunate to have spent time in. I realize, that even though I have not lived in Plainfield for many years now, and that although, my story is about my well-nurtured youth there; that the work of the people of this not-so-small-time town, continues on through the years, influencing more generations of families, both the long-standing and the newcomers to the community. Like me, how fortunate the youth of this wonderful town continue to be.

My Furry Friends

I wonder if being the only child for so many years, made my pets even more special to play with. There has always been a soft spot in my heart for animals. Like the connections that I made in the homes of my friends and neighbors, I also found a strong bond with, and great joy in caring for, my animal friends. Animals are a substantial part of country life. Those animals nurtured as pets, as well as those raised to sustain life and provide an income, are important to this way of life. I tended to many animals on our mini-farm throughout my childhood: cats, dogs, rabbits, chickens and roosters, sheep, goats, and horses.

The cats were countless, as I cared for both the house cats and those living as barn cats, but I am sure that I loved all of them. I'm still a cat girl today. In my very early years, living in our tiny trailer at the top of my parents' property, I had a beautiful, dark three-colored female cat, named Lady. She was supposed to be an outside cat, however that did not set well with me, so I made a hiding place at the head of my bunk bed where she could sleep at night. I also, pilfered a little food and milk to help her sleep through the night. After all, I always had a bedtime snack. When Lady decided that it was a great spot to have her kittens, my little secret was soon discovered. I'm sure after a shower of tears, my parents finally relented, and Lady became my permanent roommate. Loving a lot of cats, also meant a lot of heartache. To this day, when I lose a pet cat, I swear no more. Yet somehow, I always find room in my heart and in my home, for another one in need of love.

I also cared for many dogs throughout my childhood, my special ones were Judy, a German shepherd, Johnny, a mongrel, Sweet Pea, a beagle, and Herman, a basset hound. In the late 1960's, my father decided that we should raise bloodhounds to show and breed. I was tasked with feeding them, which inevitably led to the next task of cleaning out the dog runs. Not So Much Fun! I did enjoy training the bloodhounds for dog shows, and earned many ribbons, trophies, etc., especially with our best show dog, Miss Nate. Gentle Old Duke, was our breed dog. After this business endeavor, I was pretty much cured of dog ownership. My poor kids only had a couple of dogs over the years. My daughter, Tracey, and granddaughter, Brittany, have more than made up for it, they are both major dog lovers. My son, Cory, followed in my footsteps and enjoys the company of cats.

I have never really been fond of having birds around, except my nana's parakeet Charlie. When I stayed overnight with Grandpa and Nana Sawyer, in their New Moon trailer, in Woodstock, Charlie would lay an egg for my breakfast. I would only eat an egg, if my friend, Charlie would lay it for me. Sure enough when I got up in the morning, I would find a hot, ready to eat, hard boiled egg in a pretty little bowl, sitting in Charlie's cage. My nana was pretty sly. Charlie was a rather small parakeet and those eggs seemed so big, how could he possibly have laid that egg? Poor Charlie!

My parents raised chickens and roosters, they were not too high on my short list of likable birds. They liked to chase me around the yard, jump on my back, and peck at me. Did I really look like chicken feed? If all of that was not terrifying enough, then there was the slaughtering process, held like some bizarre ritual each fall. Oh My! It's a wonder that I ever slept.

After cats, my second pet love, was horses. Over the course of the years, I owned many ponies and horses. They came in all sizes and temperaments. My dad and I used to attend auctions at J.W. Barber's, on the Miracle Mile, in Lebanon. One time, I fell in love with a black stud pony that was blind in one eye. My father did not bid high enough to buy him, fifty dollars was a lot of money, and off went "my" pony. I cried all the way home, all night, and into the next morning. Soon, my dad set out, hunting for a blind pony and by nightfall I had my Racer. I believe, that it cost him a little more than what the bid went for. Racer ran like the wind, was wild as hell, and eventually had to go because my parents thought that he was going to hurt me. My uncle Caleb, also a horse lover, owned Rocket, a beautiful tan and white pinto mare, with a gentle disposition and a desire to be loved by a little girl, Viola. We were a perfect match, Rocket needed a home, and I was more than willing to oblige. Rocket eventually had a colt, a stud with the same colors, and I of course, named him Astronaut.

We were lucky to have owned a horse buggy. It was a two-seater, with a standing area behind the seat, and it had high wooden spoke wheels. We also owned a simple winter horse sleigh. My parents and I, and in later years, my sister, would hook up the season appropriate mode of transportation and head into the village, to show off Rocket's adeptness at pulling us along. Afterwards, Rocket was always rewarded with a nice brushing and a generous bucket of grain.

With all pet ownership, come the responsibilities, that go with caring for another living creature. Horses were a lot of work. There were those long, hot, snake-filled days, working in the hay fields to earn their hay. They also needed exercising and grooming; as well as, feeding and watering at least twice daily, which included lugging huge pails full of water up the hill, from the house to the barn, in sun, rain, sleet, or snow. Lastly, there was the never ending "pleasant" job of mucking out the stalls. Wheelbarrow after wheelbarrow of that sweet aroma!

My Love For Speed

My adventurous side was always waiting to be tickled, by something new and exciting. Like most kids growing up, I couldn't wait to get behind the wheel of anything motorized. I was luckier than most, to have had a wide range of driving experiences, that fulfilled my love for speed.

My penchant for speedy, motorized machines likely began in my pre-school days of playing cars with my friends, Scotty and Danny MacLeay, in our dirt driveway. We made long graded tracks in the dirt, to operate our metal cars and trucks on, as well as, my special International Harvester tractor set. We of course, all the while, added the necessary sound effects. No plastic cars for us, just the real deal. Imagination galore, there were garages, parking lots, hills, and curves to maneuver. We graduated when their dad, bought a neat, little, white go-cart for the boys. In those days, you could definitely include me as one of the "boys." They blazed trails out behind their house that led us through the woods, where we whizzed around and around, wishing that our turn would never end. I see the same gleam in my grandson, Bryce's eyes, when he's playing with his cars and riding his bike.

In the mid 1960's, my dad worked on weekend nights at the Go-Cart track in Hartland, Vermont, where my family would go to watch the races. There were also times when kids could rent the carts to test their skills behind the wheel. I was around ten years old, and most of the boys renting go-carts were teenagers. My days of practice on the MacLeay's go-cart would soon pay off. My father, would adjust the governor on my go-cart, so that it would run faster than the others. Didn't I just love waving at those teen boys, as I left them in my dust on that old dirt track, lined with bales of hay for safety. The safety standards were a little less stringent in those days. This all led me to owning my very own go-cart, a bright red little number, with a roll bar and all. I drove it in circles on our lawn so much, that it cut down on the lawn mowing. Perhaps, my father had this in mind when he purchased it for me.

When Grandpa and Nana Sawyer, moved from Woodstock to Quechee, Vermont, in the mid 1960's, their new home sat across from the entrance to Interstate 89, which had just been built, but was not yet open. My grandfather was a great builder of and skillful tinker on all types of machines. Let's now, take that previously promised ride on my wizard bike, that my grandpa built for me. He took me and my wizard bike over to the entrance ramp, and onto the newly paved, but not yet traveled highway lanes of Interstate 89, and let me "rip the strip" on my mean machine. No helmet required back then, just the wind in my long hair. I was the envy of all of the teenage boys, who lived in the area. I also hung out with these guys, playing ice hockey and spending hours on the snowmobile trails in Vermont, stopping to cook-out over open campfires that we built in the snow, and just feeling free. My need for speed was also fulfilled on our family snowmobile at home; exploring the fields and woods, sometimes alone, and other times with friends.

I, like so many other teens, longed to drive a car. We had a long driveway, with turn around areas on each end, so I drove whatever I could get my hands on, the tractor, our Doodlebug jalopy, the old Econoline Ford Van, and when I was lucky, my parents car. Up and down, and around that long drive, I would go. Gas must have been much cheaper then. I think that everyone should learn to drive on a standard stick.

My first car was a cream colored Pontiac Bonneville. Going to high school in Lebanon, meant a lot of traveling back and forth, for the Plainfield students. Lee Raymond and I, and others, put a lot of miles on that car. Playing sports, attending school activities, and social events required several trips a week and traveling in all types of weather. Driving the treacherous stretch of road through the steeply climbing and winding curves of Ward's Woods, between Plainfield and Lebanon, was a challenge to all, say nothing of a new learner. I reflect now on the responsibility, that both my parents and I took on, with all of the kids that I transported over the years as a teenage driver.

Soon after getting my driver's license, I managed to convince my parents to let me have that Bridgestone 90cc motorcycle. Again, the lawn took a beating while I was trying to master the art of shifting with my foot, using the accelerator on the handlebars, and all the while keeping the bike upright. I wasn't always successful at this, once, I managed to dump the bike and went flying over the windshield, which left a not-so-pretty pattern on my thigh. What protective gear? Like the good horseback rider that I was, I got right back up, and mounted that steed again. I might have been showing off a little that day.

I believe my need for speed, ended when my children were getting their driver's licenses. Funny how that works.

Weekend Fun

So much of our lives involved having fun with the land and the people who lived on it. Whether it was a day of adventure with water, or enjoying ourselves at another place in nature's playground, we understood that fun, really was, what we made of a situation and by using what was available to us. Unlike today, there was not a large selection of places that had commercial entertainment, that we could go to. It was not a daily treat, or even a weekly pleasure to go somewhere that cost money. I have many wonderful memories of those places that we did go to, as a special treat. Some that no longer exist, or if they do, they are a rarity, or are significantly different from the times that I experienced them, while I was growing up.

Finances were always tight, so eating out was a luxury, not a part of the regular weekly schedule. Deciding what restaurant we should go to, and eat at was pretty simple. The choices we had were few, but mostly memorable. I doubt the youth of today will look back on their times of going out to eat, with the same sentiments that I have of these special times and places. By the way, I'm not sure that take-out was even in our vocabulary. I've been searching my memory, and I can't ever remember going to pick up food from a restaurant and bringing it home to eat, not even a pizza. I do recall however, that during the summer months that my father would periodically go to West Lebanon, on a Friday afternoon, to meet a fish truck that had traveled to the coast, and then returned with a variety of fresh seafood to sell from the truck. Sounds great, right? He would purchase a very large bag (perhaps 5 or even 10lbs) of fresh, whole shrimp. My dad, was not a big drinker, but he would also pick-up a plastic bag of long-neck-beer bottles, I think Pabst Blue Ribbon or Old Milwaukee--strange how they came packaged this way and not in cardboard six-pack containers. Home he would come, all smiles. Guess who got to clean the shrimp? I stood at the sink for what seemed like hours, washing the shrimp, snapping their heads off, stripping out their ugly veins, and removing the shells from that glorious catch. My hands looked like prunes and itched like crazy. Have you ever heard someone say, that if you prepare a meal, it doesn't taste as good as if someone else had made it?

My first experience with fast food, was on a trip in the early 1960's, to Massachusetts to visit family. On the way, we stopped at a Howdy's Beef Burgers. Imagine a fifteen cent burger, I think my parents spent about one dollar on the three of us, for burgers, fries, and a soda. That puts a whole new face on "the value meal." I looked forward to those road trips, even more, after our discovery of the Howdy boy. "Dad, maybe we can go to one of my favorite amusement parks in Springfield and eat at Howdy's, too. Please!" I searched for that big boy, Howdy, just like the kids of today never miss those Golden Arches.

The next closest experience to fast food, was the A&W Drive-In Restaurant, offering burger baskets and draft root beer floats, served ice cold, in heavy glass "frosty mugs" with a long spoon and straw. Your meal was delivered to you on a tray that hooked over your partially open car window. The smell of that root beer was enough to make anyone drool. When I was a teenager, I took a job car-hopping at the West Lebanon A&W. I got so sick of that sweet root beer smell, that it was a long time before I enjoyed a root beer again. How I wish I could have one of those root beer floats right now.

When I was young, my family frequently went to Windsor, Vermont, to visit with friends, shop and do errands, or take me to my tap dance class, which was held in a house located on the small street behind the diner, that was once also called Main Street. Sometimes, we would also stop at one of the eateries. "Do I get to choose this time?" The Windsor Diner, which was a classic diner, complete with the juke box filled with the latest hits. I ate there, at times with my parents, as well as, on a few occasions with my church youth group. How we loved to put our coins into the table top jukebox, and sing along to our favorite hit singles. I would also look forward, to the times that we would visit Vi's Lunch. The owner, Viola Dimmick and I, were both happy to meet another Viola. Naturally, her diner held a very special place in my heart. Another hot spot, that I enjoyed stopping at was Nap's Lunch in the center of town, which was also once a favorite haunt of J. D. Salinger, where it is reported that he went to study the local teens.

Heading north, some of my other favorite spots to eat at, were the Nu-Bridge Restaurant, on the Miracle Mile and the Riverside Grill, on Route 4 in Lebanon. They both served great seafood, but when I was really young, I always ordered a hot dog, then I got wise with age. My parents hosted my second birthday party at the Nu-Bridge Restaurant. I likely didn't get served a plate of delicious fried seafood on that occasion, but I would sure like to make up for it now. My mind wanders back to laden trays, heading toward our table, the aroma of what was coming would arrive well before the food actually reached the table. I can't end this without mentioning Lander's restaurant that came along in later years, it served fantastic food. We celebrated many special events there, including my cousin Bev's wedding reception, and my grandparents' forty-fifth wedding anniversary. I also, went on a lot of dinner dates there as a young woman. My favorite dessert was their Syrian pastry. To die for!

The drive-in movie theaters were a weekend highlight, during the summer months. My family frequented the theaters in White

River Junction and in Claremont, and also in Ascutney, before it became known for it's "specialty" movies, of the X-rated kind. The car would be loaded up with pillows and blankets and away we would go. Admission was reasonable, sometimes one fee for the whole carload. If not, how many people can fit in the trunk? The car was parked in a prime spot for viewing, resting the front end of the car on the small, dirt mound, ensuring a clear line of sight over the cars in front of you. First stop, the playground. The children spilled out from the cars and headed for the merry-go-round, teeter-totters, and all of the other fun playground equipment. "Come back when it starts to get dark." At dusk, the car horns would blow, signaling everyone's anxiousness to get the big screen rolling. The speaker box would hang on the car window, with the cord, sometimes barely reaching the car. The speaker would need adjusting until the "perfect" sound emitted from it. The gigantic movie screen flickered on with scratchy lines, that we hoped would clear quickly, so as not to miss the cartoons and the mouth watering ads for the concession stand. "Don't forget to come get our steamed hot dogs, juicy burgers, hot crispy french fries, ice cold soft drinks, we also have a plentiful choice of candy and ice cream." I can't wait! "Ten minutes to show time!" The count down begins and so do the cartoons. "Five minutes to show time and don't forget the hot buttery popcorn, get it now before the show!" More cartoons and then one minute to go. Don't ever fall asleep during the first movie of the double feature, because you don't want to miss intermission. Then the time finally arrived, after you stood in the long line to the bathroom, you then stood in line at the concession stand and filled that cardboard box full of all of those advertised treats, and you didn't have to empty your wallet to do it. I cringe as I write this next line, but here it goes. When you were finished eating, you threw the empty containers out of the car window. I also have to admit, it was pretty common practice to litter back then. How could we have been so blind to such a horrific practice?

After the second picture show, the cars would line up to exit out of the dusty lot with car lights still off, kids usually sound asleep in the backseat, and oh yeah, don't forget to hang the speaker box back on the post. I would be curious to know how many cords were ripped off of those speaker stands over the years. Fortunately, the drive-ins lasted long enough, so that my husband and I, could treat our kids to this experience as well. I wonder how many still exist.

As teenagers, not only did we enjoy both the outdoor and indoor movies, but like most teens we loved our music, as well. School dances were heavily attended, and for us country kids, we enjoyed kicking up our heels to square dances in the area's halls and barns. Have you ever been to a barn dance? Like most dances, the walls were lined with chairs filled with anxious dancers, listening to the local country dance bands calling out the popular songs, waltzes, polkas and square dance calls of the those days. The dance hall floor was large and offered plenty of room for all. Sometimes, sawdust would be laid down to make the floor easier to dance on. Often the dancers were dressed in colorful outfits, with married partners often matching each other. They were among the many faithful followers, who traveled the countryside each Saturday night, to hear their favorite players. Both my mother's and my generation, loved to dance to the sounds of Leon Woodward and his "Woody and the Ramblers." Now do-sa-do your corner, swing your partner, and promenade, all the way home.

Record hops, also called street dances were never missed. Ours were held in the school's front parking lot. The DJ spun the records, while couples danced, and contests were held. Ronnie Slayton and I won first prize, a 45rpm record each, for the best Twist. I was pretty puffed up with that feat. Besides Rock-n-Roll, we all loved to move our feet and arms to "Do the Freddie," "The Mashed Potato," " The Pony," " The Monkey", and of course "The Swim."

We held some great house parties during our teen years. The Dunham home, across from the store, where countless kids could be seen, was the home to some of these parties. My friend and classmate, Richard Dunham's mother, Ellie, was always smiling, even though her house was being overrun by teens of all ages. Many house parties were also held in the basement of our home, we'd decorate with colored, paper creche streamers, and prepare lots of snacks. "Who's bringing the dip? No, not your boyfriend! I mean the chips and dip." Let the fun begin, crank up the music, turn down the lights, and dance the night away. Anyone up for a game of "Spin the Bottle" or "Post Office?" I don't even want to think about what games they play today.

Local churches in Windsor and West Lebanon held Coffee Houses for teens. They set up tables café style in their basements, served refreshments, and had live bands for our dancing pleasure. I can't remember if they charged a fee or not, but I'm sure, that the events were intended to boost their youth ministry program, and provide a reasonably priced, safe, and fun environment for the local teens.

How do teens and their parents afford the pricey cost of entertainment today? Popcorn alone, breaks the bank.

Plainfield Community Church
Photo taken by my father

Plainfield Grange Hall
Photo taken by my father

Viola and her Teddy Bear at the Valentine's Day
Social Box Luncheon in the Plainfield Grange Hall

153

Plainfield Town Hall
Photo taken by my father

My son Cory wearing his 6th grade play costume
borrowed from the Plainfield Town Hall

Mothers' and Daughters' Clubhouse
Photo Taken by my father

Philip Read Memorial Library
Photo taken by my father

Meriden Grange Hall--note the metal tube fire escape on back
Photo taken by my father

Inside Plainfield General Store - Old Post Office and mailboxes
Glass Candy Counter-right front
Photo Courtesy of Mary-Jo (Barto) Straus

Viola's second Birthday Party with family--5 generations shown
At Nu-Bridge Restaurant, Miracle Mile, Lebanon, NH

Viola and her cat Lady with her kittens

A Look Ahead

As happens in life, we grow up and move on. We meet new friends, face new challenges, and life takes over. We have families and careers that require our attention and time. Like me, many store the memories of their childhood deep within them, and take a peek at them when our minds are jogged by a certain event, or when we are lucky enough to spend time with an old acquaintance or friend.

The years passed, and the times changed. The Cornish Colony, was not what it once was, but there were still some families who came back for the summer, and instead of playing in some of these beautiful homes, now in my late teen years, I was now working in them. In the early 1970's, my cousin, Bev (Wilder) Widger and her husband, Bob, and I, used to work on occasion for these families, preparing for and serving at their dinner parties. The parties were sometimes small intimate gatherings, and at other times, large, festive affairs. The house would be cleaned, the dining room set with a beautifully arranged table, and the meal cooked, as instructed. One time, I had to garnish a large piece of baked fish, to make it look like a fish--head to tail, fins included. I used black olives and vegetables to create my masterpiece. By the way, I left off the hook, line, and sinker. When the evening social hour began, we served the guests hors d'oeuvres and cocktails that were prepared by us. Later, we served the dinner from first to last course, and then the cleanup began in earnest. When we were finished with our work, it looked like the party had never happened, with everything neatly returned to its rightful place, until the next time. We were sometimes entertained along with the guests, by the musical talents of one of the attendees. It is sad to see so many of these grand places now sitting idle. Call me, I'm up for returning and putting on a dinner party or two, in one of these beautiful homes.

My story led me to Lebanon High School, where I was introduced to more great teachers, more friends, and memories galore. Then off to college, at the University of New Hampshire, and then, finally settling on a career in Criminal Justice, earning a Bachelor of Science degree from St. Anselm College. My internship, as a Juvenile Justice Officer, at the Claremont Police Department, led to new doors opening, and to my rewarding career in Corrections.

I also was blessed with a loving husband and two precious children, who have supported me in all that I have chosen to do, and they continue to offer me love and strength today, with the addition of their spouses, and my dear grandchildren.

With all of this richness in my life, I realize that the foundation of who I am today, lies in the community of my not-so-small-time town, Plainfield.

All Goods Things Must End

As I reach the end of my story, I struggle hard with the fact that I have left so many out. Truly, the whole story of our not-so-small time town, Plainfield, does include each and every person, who touched my life during those years. However, reality sets in, and I realize that it is an impossibility to be all encompassing, and how much does the reader really have time for, as the story is almost endless.

I find myself walking down to the village on my well traveled Westgate Road, passing by the small trailer where Glen Small quietly lived his life, and seeing Mr. Garrand and Mr. Amidon working in their yards and tending to their gardens. They were never too busy to wave and say hi, as I passed by walking, riding my bike, or on horseback. The Adams boys and my buddy, Graydon Gile, Jr. and his sisters, were more of my friends that I spent much time with. The Morse home, was always filled with Sookie's beautiful music, and his yard iced over into a great hockey rink, for us kids to use in the winter. Hayward Road would lead you to Stone's Meat Market if you needed a choice cut of meat. On the corner of Hayward, was the Gibson home, where Joe Gibson lived, he was our resident State Police Officer, in their driveway sat his cruiser with a bubble gum light, sitting on its roof. Their next door neighbors were, my snowball partner, Mr. Bennett and his wife. Fred and Barbara Sweet's home is where their daughter, Judy, babysat for me and we listened to " Itsy, Bitsy, Teenie, Weenie, Yellow, Polka-Dot Bikini" and other 45's in their living room, until we almost wore out the vinyl grooves. The Maylin's small cottage home is where Ellen wrote her articles about the local news for the newspapers, and worked on her stamp collection. She, as well as my father and I, belonged to the Plainfield Stamp Collecting Club. I specialized in bird stamps, go figure, with my aversion back in those days to those feathery creatures, except, of course for Nana's Charlie. I must have thought that those beautifully colored creatures looked just fine on stamps, where they couldn't flutter their wings at me. The Renihan home, with its elegant yard sat at the end of the road. This property was owned by the Hanks in earlier years. On the opposite corner is where the Stettenheims, Peter and Sandy, moved into the former home of the Pearsons, which was once, also occupied by members of the Cornish Colony. I babysat for their children, Wendy and Joel, and did housekeeping for them. My imagination worked over time, as I cleaned the rooms of that large and beautiful home. Maybe, I was meant to be a Princess.

The Village of Plainfield, was like a painting of people sitting on their front porches. The porch scene started across the street at the end of our road, with "Grandpa and Grammy" Nicolaisen-- so called, by all. Traveling past the Bernard-Gobin home, and the hidden stone cottage where the Koehlers lived, was where you could find Vernon Hood, sitting by his wood stove in his kitchen. This was a common gathering spot for the town folk, where one could watch him smoking his pipe, while he shared his vast knowledge on so many topics. Mr. and Mrs. Pickering, everyone called him Pick, always had a cheery hello for me as I passed by their front porch. A rarity for those days, Pick was also a male nurse, who saved my mother's live one day. She cut her hand and wrist, while washing a large glass pitcher that broke, with her hand in it. As a youngster, the blood was very frightening to me, as her wound bled through the dish towel, that she had wrapped her hand in. She drove one-handed to the Pickering home, where he tended to the injury before driving us to the Windsor Hospital Emergency Room, while consoling me all the way. Harold "Pa" Hoisington and his wife, sat on their porch on the other end of the village, he was the local farrier who traveled to farms shoeing horses, including mine. The Quimby home sitting on the small hill leaving the village, overlooked the Jenny's Potato Business, which was located next to the schoolhouse. Adjacent to the Grange Hall, is where one could find Max Plummer quietly watching over the street. John Meyette's family might be sitting on the porch of their farmhouse, once the home of Ralph Jordan. From their yard, they could look past their large vegetable garden at the Northrup's, where our reading teacher once lived. The Thorntons next lived in this lovely house. Also seen on the main street, were the familiar faces of Henrietta Kenyon, Mrs. Hadley, The Waites, Marjorie Spaulding, tending to her antique shop, and Sophie Morse in her rocking chair, with her knitting needles clicking away, while she sat on the front porch of her quaint, little cottage home, a must stop to say hi, and usually score a baked treat or two.

I also find myself playing and laughing in my memories, with all of my grammar school classmates, over the years. You too, live on in my thoughts. A special shout out to Donnie Perkins, who could recite any baseball statistic recorded, and if memory serves me, he was also a pretty good marble player, too. Do you still have yours? Are you up for a rematch?

What Plainfield girl doesn't remember when those cute Longacre boys came to town, and added to the landscape of handsome young men, some already spoken of, and others including, but not limited to, Georgie Koehler, the Gobin brothers, Dickie Northrup, the Williams boys, Chris Stone, Winnie Spencer…

As you can see, and are probably hoping that I will not, I could go road by road, naming each household, and have a little tidbit to share in how they added to the years of my youth, that I was so fortunate to have lived in this wonderful town. I will stress again that everyone mentioned, or not, made our very special Plainfield, a not-so-small-time town.

My wish is that there will be endless generations of children as fortunate as me, to frolic in the Blow-Me-Down Brook and other swimming holes, build snow forts and have snowball fights, ride horseback, enjoy those beautiful old buildings, and make friends new and old, that will last a lifetime. May they always be able to look back fondly on all of the special people who touched their lives, while growing up in our not-so-small-time town, Plainfield, New Hampshire, with its glorious landscape and rich history.

In Special Memory

My baby sister, Carol, was taken from us at the early age of thirty-one, after having survived seven years of treatment for, and the side effects from, a malignant brain tumor. In some respect, her life as she knew it, really ended at the age of twenty-four. She too, was fortunate to have lived in the very special, not-so-small-time town, Plainfield. Even though her experiences were ten years later than mine, some different and some the same, I know how much she enjoyed hers as well. I know that if she had written her story, it would also have been hard to include each person that touched her life. Thanks to everyone who did. I will share a couple of my thoughts.

The family of Bill and Merilyn Smith served as her second home, where she had wonderful times with Deena, her best friend Stephanie "Stevie", who my son had a crush on, Erica, and Billy. I believe that their stories might be a bit more wild, than mine. Although, I might have left out a couple of things to protect the "innocent." Scott Martin and Billy Dow, were like brothers to her. She too, had close family interactions and special cousins to play with.

Mrs. Corette, Denis Reisch, and Steve and Donna Beaupré, would for sure be in her story. Malcolm Grobe would be her hero, and indeed was, right up to her last breath. He was also our savior, as he helped us lay her to rest.

Gary K
423-312-0098

Made in United States
Orlando, FL
03 October 2022

22934616R00114